THE FU[   ]
G[   ]
PLAYING POOL

BY JON DENN
COLBURN PRESS, MONTVALE, NEW JERSEY

UNANIMOUS PRAISE

"Can there be higher praise? Delightful... ingenious!"
George Fels (Author of Mastering Pool -and- Pool
Simplified...Somewhat), <u>BILLIARD DIGEST</u>

"A great deal of work went into the book and the care
and attention to detail pays off. A very solid technical
foundation...the information is accurate and revealed in
a way that builds on the previous chapters. Worthy of
your time."
Tom Shaw, <u>POOL AND BILLIARD MAGAZINE</u>

"...A fresh approach to the basics." <u>AMERICAN CUEIST</u>

"Chock full of information...and F-U-N ! ...a *MUST BUY*.
Succinctly, Denn has found the secret to an
instructional author's success-keep it simple."
<u>NATIONAL BILLIARD NEWS</u>

Originally titled "Rack 'Em Daddy!"

COLBURN PRESS
P.O. BOX 356
MONTVALE, NEW JERSEY 07645

DESIGNED AND ILLUSTRATED BY JON DENN,
ADDITIONAL ILLUSTRATIONS BY RON SR.,
RON JR. AND CHRIS CARLUCCI, AND KEVIN MILLER.

MANUFACTURED IN THE UNITED STATES
ISBN 0-9634187-4-2
LIBRARY OF CONGRESS CATALOG CARD NUMBER
UNDER ORIGINAL TITLE
92-73955
DENN, JON
RACK 'EM DADDY!
ISBN 0-96344187-5-0
10 9 8 7 6 5 4 3

DEDICATED TO WENDY DENN, MY WIFE,
ROBERT AND BARBARA DENN , MY PARENTS

AND

TO POOL -- THE SPORT .

ABOUT THE AUTHOR

Jon Denn is a certified instructor in the sport of Pool and Billiards. He is a successful room operator and has tested each lesson thoroughly for your enjoyment. He wrote this book because of the lack of easy to understand material on the sport.

TABLE OF CONTENTS

FOREWARD

My first exposure to the sport of pool, like most youth, was the 8 foot table in the rec room of our home. My father loved the game (still does), and mother used to joke that he would come home in the evening and say hello to the table before addressing the rest of the family.

My grandfather also played, and my initial instruction in the finer points of pool was to watch them play pool, earning a dollar to rack the balls for them after each inning. The excitement of this task for a ten year old, somewhat akin to watching paint dry, made me an adamant believer that horses, and not billiards, would be my passion in life.

Until two things happened: First, my dad taught me how to make a few simple shots, and showed me a few rudimentary practice ideas. Second, he took me to the BCA's U.S. Open Straight Pool Championships in Chicago, where I had the opportunity to see Jean Balukas, only four years my senior, devastate a field of older and more experienced players. Seeing her, I thought to myself "heck,, I could do that", and I began to play more frequently.

As most participants in the cue sports soon learn, playing and practicing are two entirely different things, and I quickly became frustrated at how little my game seemed to improve. At the same time, my father, a talented player himself, started tinkering with a hand made instructional manual, composed of sample shots, and the resulting position for each shot, depending on the spin used on the cue ball. Each page, carefully diagrammed, was encased in plastic, bound in a three ring notebook. Suddenly I had a goal--to make the shots, and have the cue ball end up in the same places as were shown on each page--I was hooked.

Twenty years later, I have become very involved in the sport. Together with my father, Harold Simonsen, and several younger siblings, we publish Pool and Billiard Magazine, providing eager fans with tournament results, instruction, and as much information as we can gather on the sport, its players, and its equipment.

Additionally, I currently serve as President of the Billiard Education Foundation, which provides young aspiring players the opportunity to participate in the annual BCA Junior Nationals, and to travel abroad to compete in the World Junior Championships.

I also am lucky enough to compete on the women's professional billiard tour, thanks to the fundamental instruction I had as a youngster. (Though I still cannot devastate a field of older and more experienced players...yet!)

My daughter , Meegan, age seven, recently announced that she wants to play pool, "like her mom". I was naturally thrilled and flattered at her interest, but had no clue where to begin teaching her. Harold's handmade instruction book was long gone, and I was sure I hadn't the time or the patience to build another.

Thanks to Jon Denn, the Pied Piper of Pool, I won't have to.

When I first picked up this book, the thing that most impressed me weren't the cartoon characters, or the clever lines, or the amusing diagrams. What really sold me was the level of the instruction, teaching finer points of the game in such an easy manner. So many things are included-- that would've taken me months to (even figure out how to) explain to my daughter! The author has clearly captured the intrigue of the sport for the young player.

As someone who plays pool, is interested in the future of pool, and who wants my own children to fall in love with the game as I have, I can attest that this book is a great opportunity for young players to learn, but most of all, to have fun.

Shari J. Stauch, 6 June 1993

For more information about these organizations please write:

Billiard Congress of America
1700 S. 1st Avenue
Iowa City, Iowa 52240
(319) 351-2112

 and

Pool and Billiard Magazine
109 Fairfield Way, Suite 207
Bloomingdale, IL 60108

(708) 892-7828

Introduction: This is My Tune

Many of the village folk asked me to show their children (and themselves) how to play pool. So many, in fact, that I wrote down the lessons given in my own club, and made this book.

Some days you will play well, some days poorly. Remember that pool is to be enjoyed--have FUN! Enjoy the company of your friends and family. Do your best to play consistently and with the same system.

Someone once asked me what "Pied" meant. To me, it is like a piece of pie. It is the portion of the pool table that will give you a good play on the next ball.

Pool is a lifetime sport. By learning how to play well now, you will be able to play well forever. Great play takes lots of practice and commitment. However, very good play can be maintained with regular visits to a table. Knowing the basics will also allow you to get back into the game after a long absence.

There are many aspects of the game that only a rare person can figure out by oneself. These have to do with the way physical things react to each other. This is called physics. You will learn more about physics from Marshal Newton and others in this book.

Billiards is another name for pool. Billiards also has many meanings. It can be a cue sport played with three balls on a table with no pockets. It is also what happens when the cue ball leaves the object ball and before it comes to rest (also known as a carom).

It is long past the time for pool to be elevated to its rightful place in the great body of sport. Please, promise to teach your children well so they do not take their natural curiosity to a hustler. Hustling is stealing. Gambling with a stranger is dangerous. Gambling with an acquaintance is empty. Gamble with a friend and lose a friend.

I am a keeper of promises, so if you do not understand any part of this book-- write to me and I will do my best to explain it better. This Pied Piper will return the children to you understanding that it is how you play the game that counts.

Have a great time in the Land of Pool.   Jon Denn   10 July 1992

PROLOGUE

Once upon a time, in the Land of Pool, lived a fine Cue Stick. This grey Cue Stick was a little worn, but was made of fine hard wood. When rolled on the table its ferrule (kind of a hat that the leather tip sits on) stayed flush on the table. The other Cue Sticks laughed at the grey Cue Stick because they were shiny and new, not grey at all.

Not many players chose "Grey" to use when playing pool. One day a quiet boy chose Grey. Grey was delighted and the boy did well. Many days thereafter the boy visited the Land of Pool and tossed the grey Cue Stick. Together they took a wondrous journey and learned how to play pool well.

The boy is now a man and still tosses the grey Cue Stick. He's called the "Pied Piper" and the Cue Stick the "Grey Ghost". Join them now for exciting adventures in and around the Land of Pool.

The Land that time nearly misunderstood.

ACKNOWLEDGMENTS

Many thanks to the following people for the development of this book:
To Anthony Dragona for the insight into the educators' point of view and technical assistance. To R.J. Gillens and Kim Haagen for the endless conversations about the process and their creative solutions to those thorny little problems. Extra thanks to R.J. for "Eek*wal's Song". To Joe Cotrupe for proofing the table diagrams. To Dick Bertan for last minute assistance in the production process. To Ron Sr., Chris and Ron Jr. Carlucci for the human cartoon characters . To Kevin Miller for the hand drawings.

Finally, thanks to Wendy Denn for moral support during the process.

Some table illustrations have, for the sake of clarity, exaggerated features. In other cases, the cut of the pockets has been altered or the balls have been enlarged to show detail.

Use these diagrams as guides for the content of the issue on that page.

I highly recommend these other fine books
FELS, MASTERING POOL
BYRNE'S STANDARD BOOK OF POOL AND BILLIARDS
MARTIN, 99 CRITICAL SHOTS
THE BCA, OFFICIAL RULES AND RECORDS BOOK
KOEHLER , THE SCIENCE OF POCKET BILLIARDS
MIZERAK WITH PANOZZO, COMPLETE BOOK OF POOL.

THE PIED PIPER'S--

THEY ALL RACK UP CHARACTER, TOO.

AAR**ON** Q

KWAN TYM

YOU CAN CALL ME PIPER. THANKS AND WELCOME.

PIPER NOTE **LOOK FOR MY NOTES.**

SUZY Q

YOU Q

TOP Q

--POOL PLAYERS

THEY WILL SHOW YOU --THE LAND OF POOL.

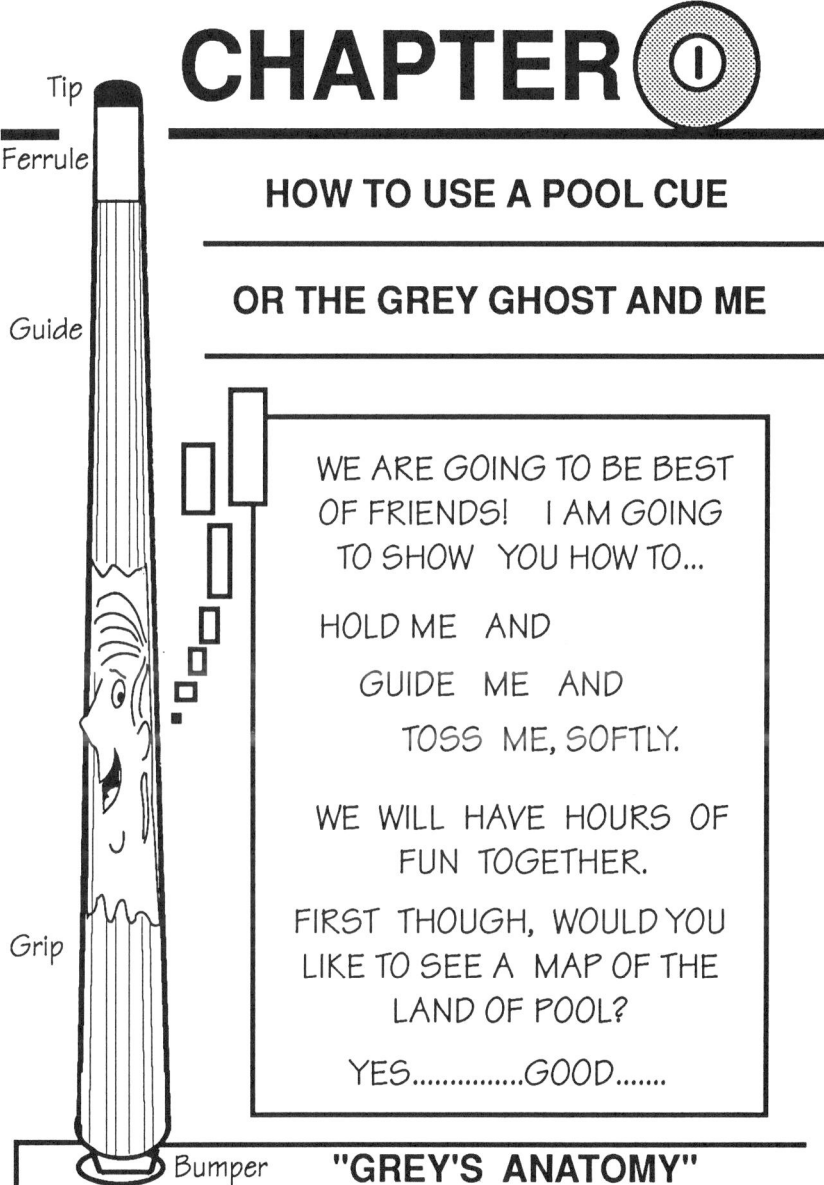

Tip

Ferrule

Guide

CHAPTER ①

HOW TO USE A POOL CUE

OR THE GREY GHOST AND ME

WE ARE GOING TO BE BEST OF FRIENDS! I AM GOING TO SHOW YOU HOW TO...

HOLD ME AND

GUIDE ME AND

TOSS ME, SOFTLY.

WE WILL HAVE HOURS OF FUN TOGETHER.

FIRST THOUGH, WOULD YOU LIKE TO SEE A MAP OF THE LAND OF POOL?

YES..............GOOD.......

Grip

Bumper   **"GREY'S ANATOMY"**

LAND OF POOL MAP-

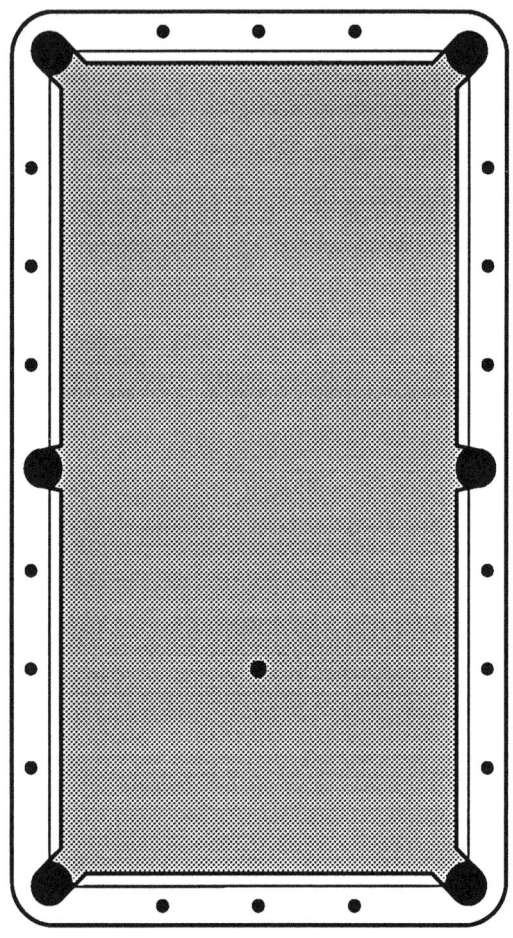

WHEN YOU STEP UP TO THE TABLE OR THINK ABOUT
THE LAND OF POOL YOU WILL NEED THIS MAP.

-AND ITS LEGEND

1. A Pool table is twice as long as it is wide. 2. It has six pockets (#1-6). 3. It has six rails also known as banks, made of rubber. The banks keep the balls from falling off the table and the rubber cushions bounce the ball back into the body of the table. 4. It has eighteen marked diamonds--three on each rail. These can be used to assist aiming and to figure out angles on banked balls. 5. The playing surface and the cushions are all covered in very fine, wool cloth.

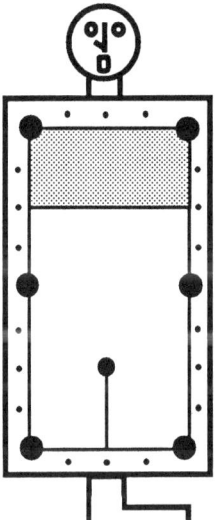

6. Some table's pockets are big. They are amateur tables.

7. Some table's pockets are small. They are professional tables.

8. The playing surface is 31 inches off the ground.

9. The head of the table is where your head is when you break.

10. Breaking is done from behind the second diamond at the head of the table (double shaded) it is called the kitchen. So if the head gets hungry...11. The foot of the table is where the racking of the balls is done. The front ball of the rack goes on the footspot which is marked for you.. 12. There is also a headspot and center spot but sometimes they are invisible. 13. The footspot's longstring are where balls are spotted.

•CLOSE-UP PROFILE•

THE POCKETS

 PIPER NOTE The Happy Jaw helps you pocket a ball.
The Unhappy Jaw usually stops you from pocketing a ball.

**... so, do bounce the ball off Happy Jaw!
Stay away from the Unhappy Jaw.
(If you can see the jaw, it's the Happy Jaw.)**

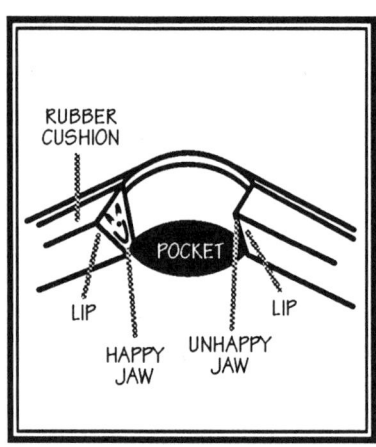

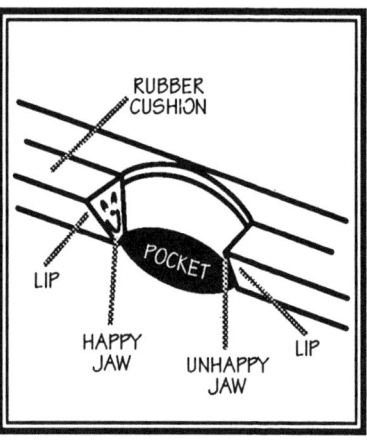

A CORNER POCKET   **A SIDE POCKET**

KEEP TALKING HAPPY JAW!!

THE MOST IMPORTANT
BALLS IN THE GAME ARE...

EYE-BALLS

HA...HA...HA....

BECAUSE YOU AIM WITH THEM.   MORE ABOUT AIMING AFTER THIS
IMPORTANT MESSAGE FROM "GREY" ON HOW TO HOLD HIM.

HOLD ME ...PLEASE... LIKE THIS...
AS FIRM AS A JUICE CAN.

MOSTLY WITH THE THUMB AND
INDEX FINGER.   JUST LAY THE
OTHER FINGERS DOWN ON MY
GRIP.

DO NOT SQUEEZE ME TOO TIGHT--
OR HOLD ME TOO LIGHT.

PIPER
NOTE

**USUALLY RIGHTIES HOLD THE CUE IN THEIR RIGHT
HAND AND LEFTIES HOLD IT IN THEIR LEFT HAND.**

HERE IS AN OPEN BRIDGE

AN OPEN BRIDGE IS A "V" BRIDGE.

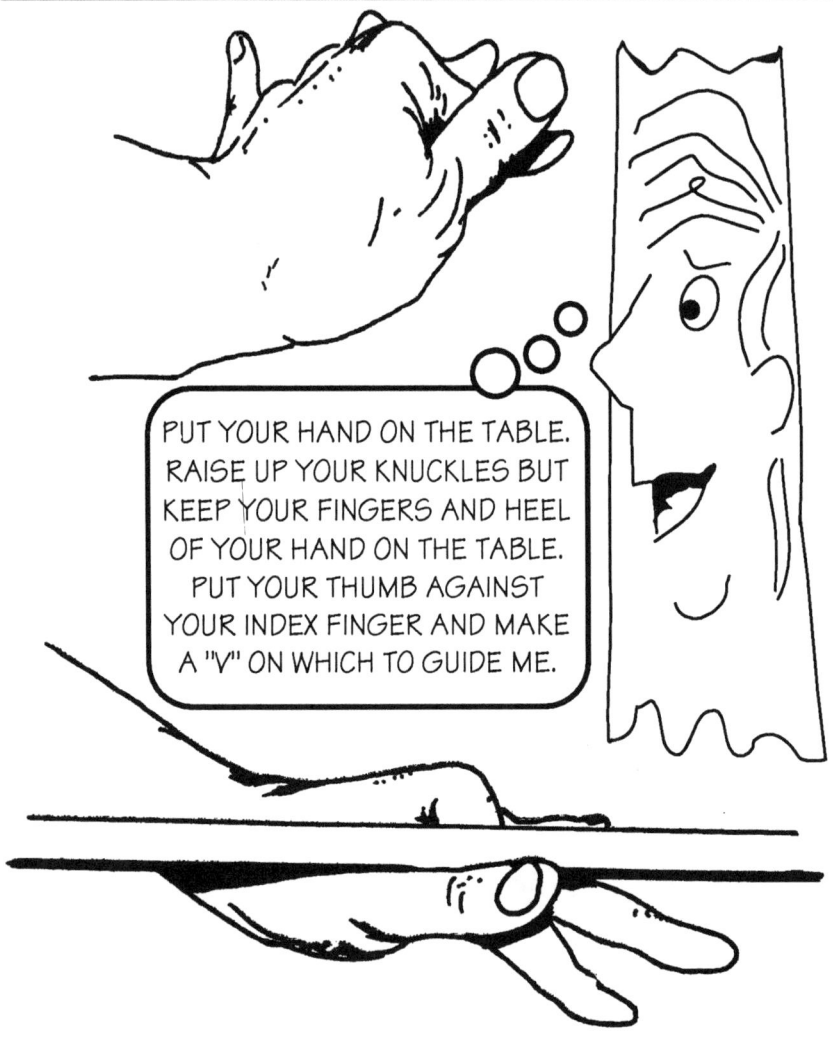

PUT YOUR HAND ON THE TABLE. RAISE UP YOUR KNUCKLES BUT KEEP YOUR FINGERS AND HEEL OF YOUR HAND ON THE TABLE. PUT YOUR THUMB AGAINST YOUR INDEX FINGER AND MAKE A "V" ON WHICH TO GUIDE ME.

PLEASE, DO NOT THROW ME HARD. JUST TOSS ME, SOFTLY

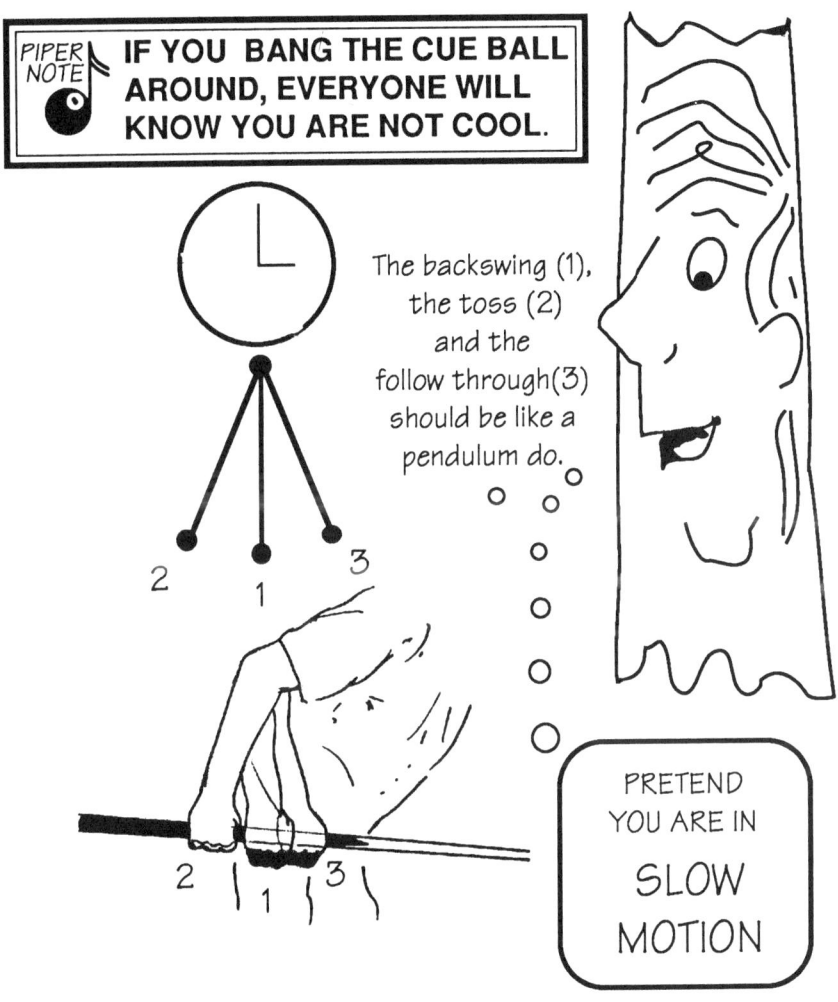

PIPER NOTE
IF YOU BANG THE CUE BALL AROUND, EVERYONE WILL KNOW YOU ARE NOT COOL.

The backswing (1), the toss (2) and the follow through(3) should be like a pendulum do.

2 1 3

2 1 3

PRETEND YOU ARE IN SLOW MOTION

GAME NUMBER ONE
SEVEN OUT OF TEN "NO TOUCH"

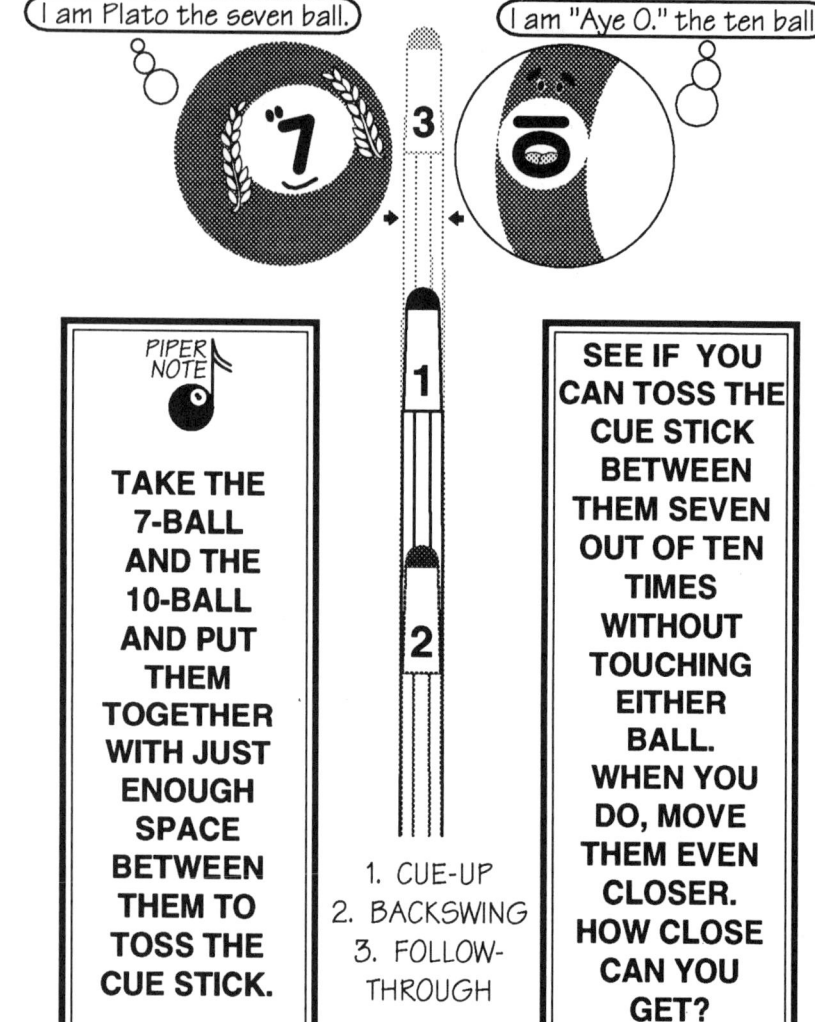

SUMMARY

I like pool. It is fun to toss the Cue Stick. I do it so well they call me Suzy Q. Remember: It is very important to hold the Cue Stick correctly. Guide it through an open bridge and toss it straight. There is nothing more important than this to play good pool. All you can do is toss the Cue Stick. Use the same speed on the backswing as the toss. Slow and easy, slow motion , follow through and freeze.

PIPER NOTE **You can practice tossing straight at home! Just make a loop target from a hanger or use the opening of a bottle as a guide. Use your Cue Stick or even a broom handle.**

"EDDY CUT" OFFERS SHOTS ON ETIQUETTE

What is Etiquette? It is the way everyone is expected to behave while they are playing pool. This way everyone can enjoy themselves. Here is one shot: Always return the Cue Stick to the wall where you found it, so the next player has a full choice.

19

CHAPTER ②

HERE IS ROCKY CONTROL--THE CUE BALL

My Left Half | My Right Half

My Top Half

HI GREY!

HI ROCKY!

My Bottom Half

I am cream color and made of phenolic resin. You need to aim at my nose. Pin the nose on Rocky with Grey-- I will show you where.

PIPER NOTE

The Cue Stick meets the Cue Ball.

Q. What if the Cue Stick glances off the Cue Ball? A. It is called a Miscue. This is a foul and you lose your turn.

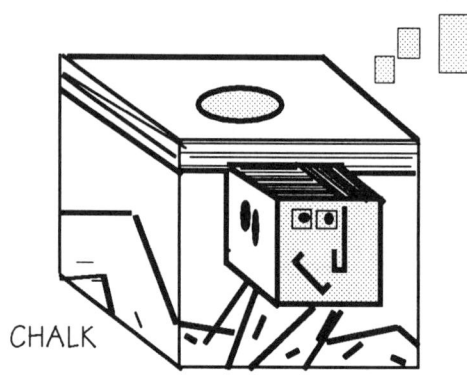

CHALK

THE CUBE IS "T. DUSTY" CHALK
--THE TABLE TROLL--

I help the Cue Stick tip grip the Cue Ball. I am the only thing that has to come between them. I help prevent miscues.

Be careful not to get little pieces of chalk on the table. They interfere with the roll of the ball and make you miss.

PIPER NOTE **CHALK THE CUE STICK'S TIP LIGHTLY BEFORE EVERY TOSS--SO IT DOES NOT SLIP OFF THE CUE BALL.**

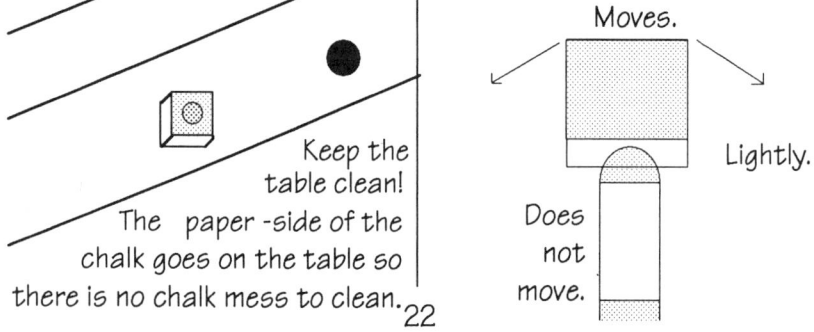

Keep the table clean! The paper -side of the chalk goes on the table so there is no chalk mess to clean.

Moves.

Lightly.

Does not move.

22

ROCKY IS A NATURAL BALL

BABY, I WAS BORN TO ROLL..

A BALL HAS GOT TO DO WHAT A BALL HAS GOT TO DO.

LET'S GET ROLLING

Both Rocky and you need to start off correctly.
Rocky needs to roll--so first you have to learn how to
control a rolling Cue Ball. Rocky can do tricks but tricks
are against Rocky's nature. Rocky will cooperate but the
Cue Ball behavior is harder to predict.

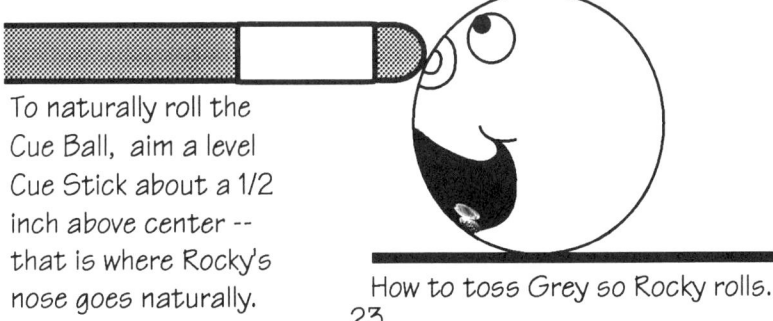

To naturally roll the
Cue Ball, aim a level
Cue Stick about a 1/2
inch above center --
that is where Rocky's
nose goes naturally.

How to toss Grey so Rocky rolls.

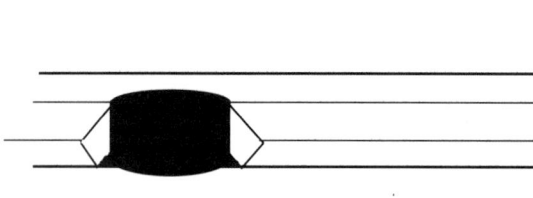

OPTICAL ILLUSION

Things are not always what
they appear to be.

You see the top of the pool
cue--not the actual point
of contact between the
Cue Tip and the Cue Ball.

THIS IS CALLED PARALLAX.
MAKE SURE YOU ARE
REALLY CONTACTING THE
CUE BALL A HALF INCH
ABOVE CENTER.

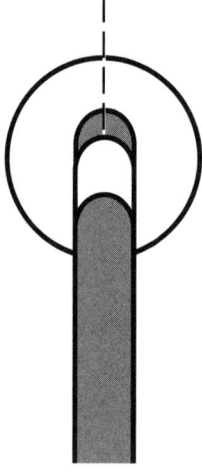

False

True

SIDE VIEW

A PROPER TOSS

BACK AND FORTH – TWO INCHES

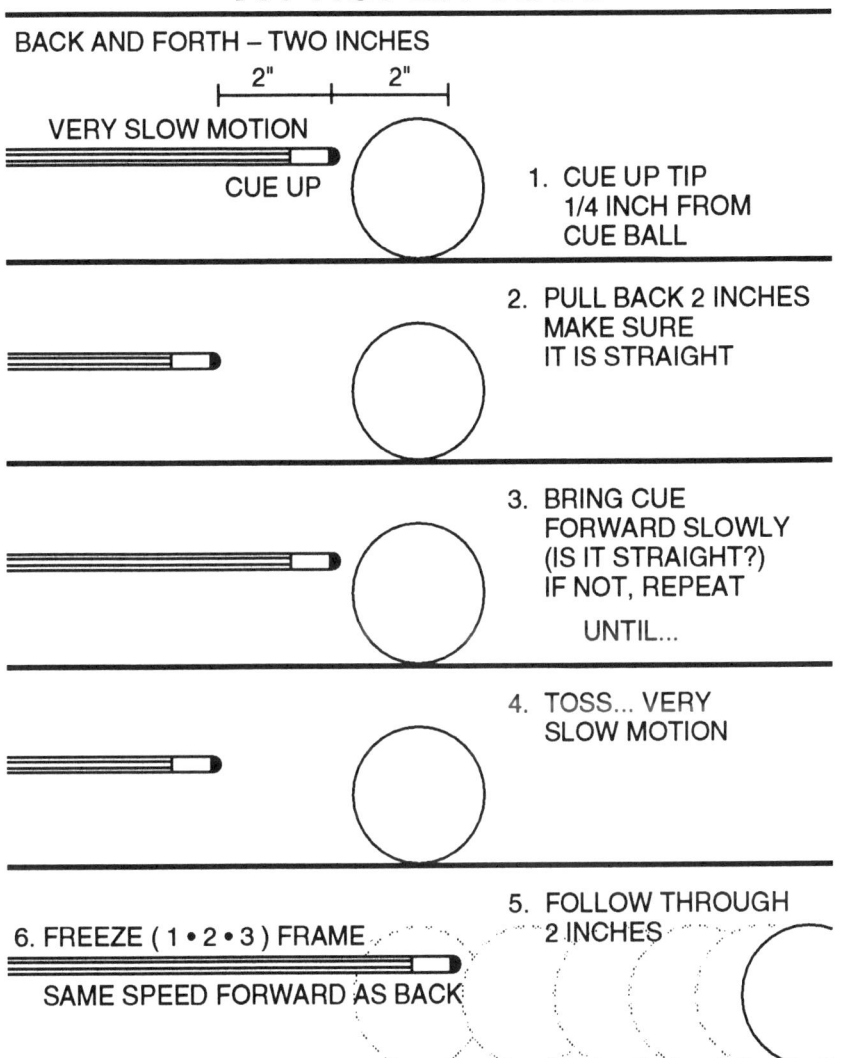

|← 2" →|← 2" →|

VERY SLOW MOTION

CUE UP

1. CUE UP TIP
   1/4 INCH FROM
   CUE BALL

2. PULL BACK 2 INCHES
   MAKE SURE
   IT IS STRAIGHT

3. BRING CUE
   FORWARD SLOWLY
   (IS IT STRAIGHT?)
   IF NOT, REPEAT

   UNTIL...

4. TOSS... VERY
   SLOW MOTION

5. FOLLOW THROUGH
   2 INCHES

6. FREEZE (1 • 2 • 3) FRAME

SAME SPEED FORWARD AS BACK

7. MEDIUM SPEED-BACK AND FORTH 3 INCHES FROM CUE UP.
8. MEDIUM FAST---BACK AND FORTH 4 INCHES FROM CUE UP.
9. FAST SPEED -- BACK AND FORTH 5 INCHES FROM CUE UP.

HOW TO BE ONE WITH THE CUE

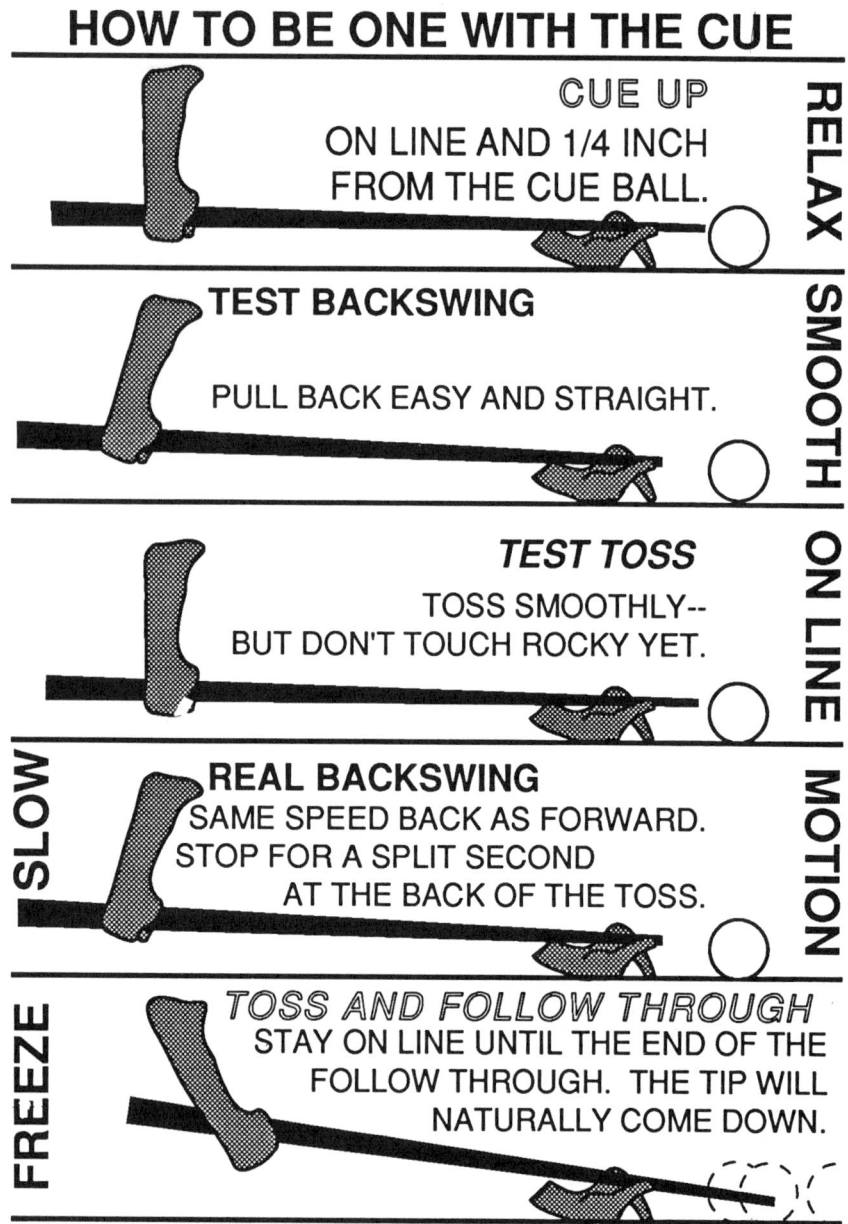

CUE UP
ON LINE AND 1/4 INCH
FROM THE CUE BALL.

RELAX

TEST BACKSWING

PULL BACK EASY AND STRAIGHT.

SMOOTH

TEST TOSS
TOSS SMOOTHLY--
BUT DON'T TOUCH ROCKY YET.

ON LINE

REAL BACKSWING
SAME SPEED BACK AS FORWARD.
STOP FOR A SPLIT SECOND
AT THE BACK OF THE TOSS.

SLOW

MOTION

TOSS AND FOLLOW THROUGH
STAY ON LINE UNTIL THE END OF THE
FOLLOW THROUGH. THE TIP WILL
NATURALLY COME DOWN.

FREEZE

GAME NUMBER TWO
TOSS STRAIGHT GAME

A great warm-up, too.

"7" Out of 10 "Bounce Back Bankshots"

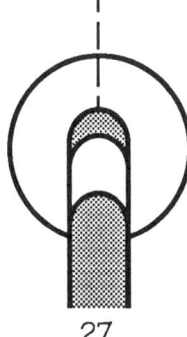

Toss the Cue Stick into the Cue Ball so it goes to the rail. After you toss the Cue Stick--Freeze. The Cue Ball must come back centered on the Cue Stick, exactly where it began..

Then try it on the length of the table. Try it at slow and medium speeds. Remember, do it Seven out of Ten times. When you win at this game you are developing a great toss!!

27

IF YOU ARE SURE YOU ARE ON LINE AND TOSSING STRAIGHT, BUT ROCKY IS NOT COMING BACK TO GREY--THEN YOU ARE NOT CONTACTING ROCKY EXACTLY ON THE LINE THAT SEPARATES HIS LEFT AND RIGHT HALVES.

SUMMARY

I am always very careful where I contact the Cue Ball. That is why they call me "On" Cue. Remember: A naturally rolling Cue Ball starts out rolling. It is the natural way to control Rocky Control. Toss on the line that separates Rocky's left and right halves about a half inch above center. There is the optical illusion to consider, too.

PIPER
NOTE

Your Cue Stick should not fly up in the air after you toss. The Cue Stick should stay sitting on the open bridge after you toss. If it does not your grip may be too tight. If the Cue Stick comes forward onto the table and raises off the bridge--you tossed really well!

"EDDY CUT" OFFERS SHOTS ON ETIQUETTE

1. Leaning on the table when your friend is playing is distracting. 2. Stand back from the table when it is not your turn, be polite, your friend is trying to play well, too.
3. Keep still if you are in your friend's line of sight, any movement is distracting.

CHAPTER

AIMING AND THE POCKETS

MEET THE POCKETS

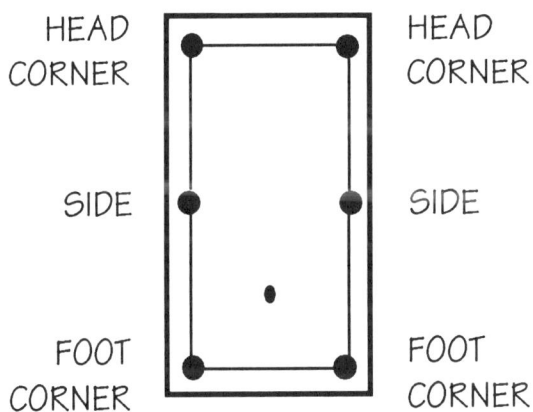

HEAD CORNER   HEAD CORNER

SIDE   SIDE

FOOT CORNER   FOOT CORNER

See if you can pocket the Cue Ball in all six pockets beginning one foot away from each. See if you can do it ten out of ten times without missing....showoff.

FOOT LONG SHOTS

FROM THE FAR FOUR

THE TUNNEL GETS SMALLER THE

 PIPER NOTE The center of the Tunnel of Smiles is where you want to aim... **NOT** at the center of the pocket.

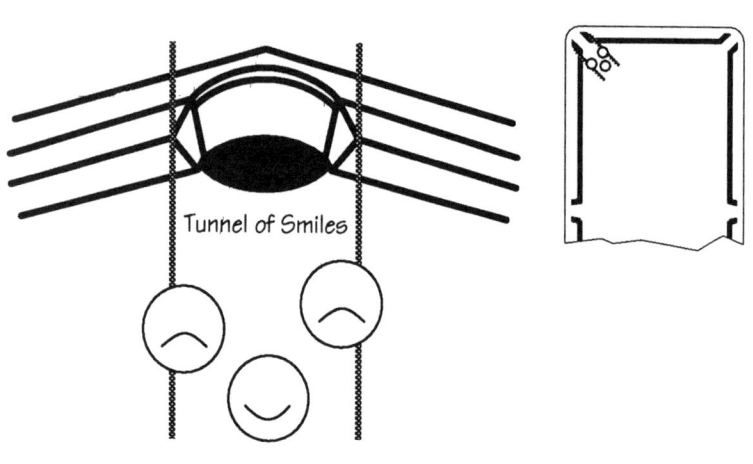

Tunnel of Smiles

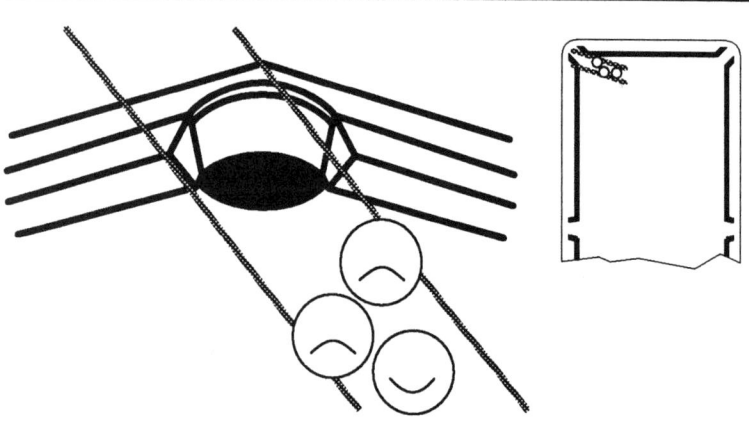

CORNERS OF THE TABLE

SHARPER THE ANGLE BECOMES

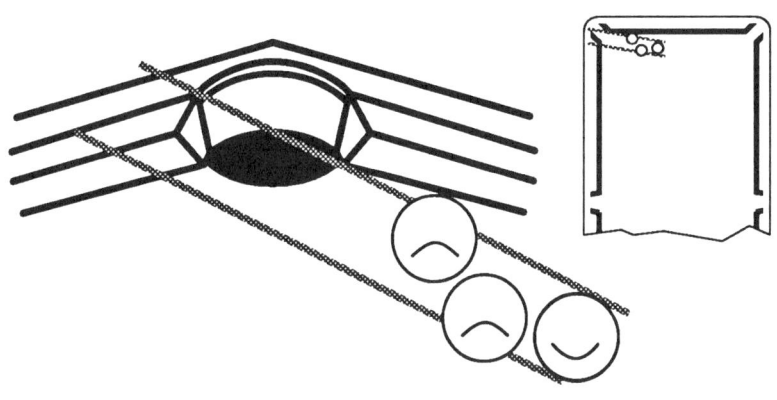

On a very sharp angle you can brush the rail to make the play.
On some tables you have to toss softer, though.

PIPER NOTE

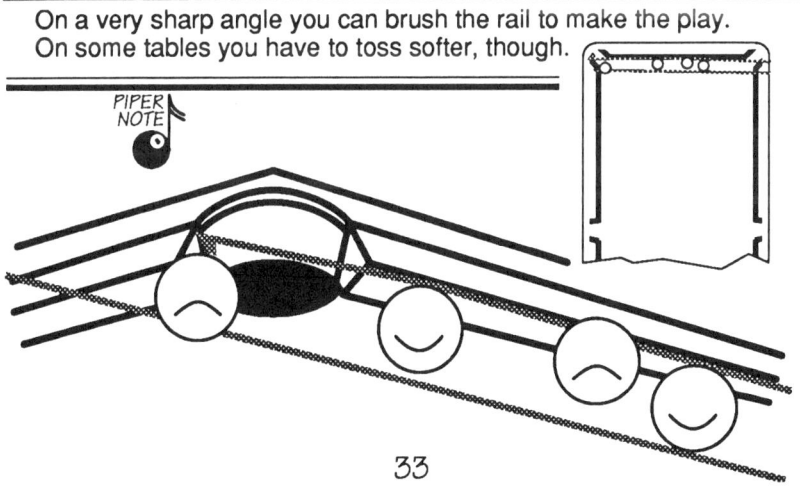

33

THERE ARE TWO SIDES-

THE TUNNEL GETS SMALLER

 PIPER NOTE The center of the Tunnel of Smiles is where you want to aim...NOT the center of the pocket.

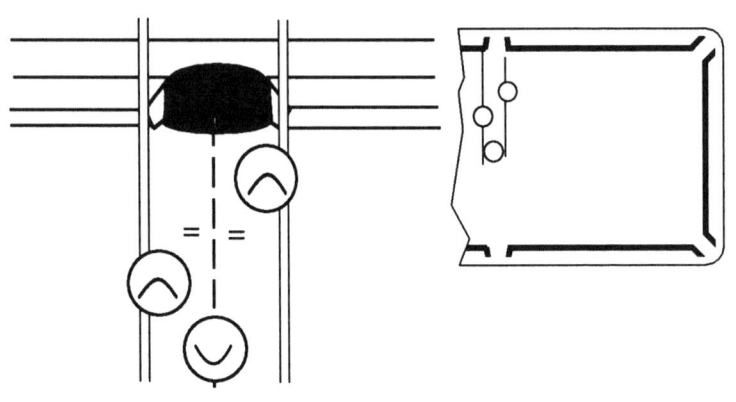

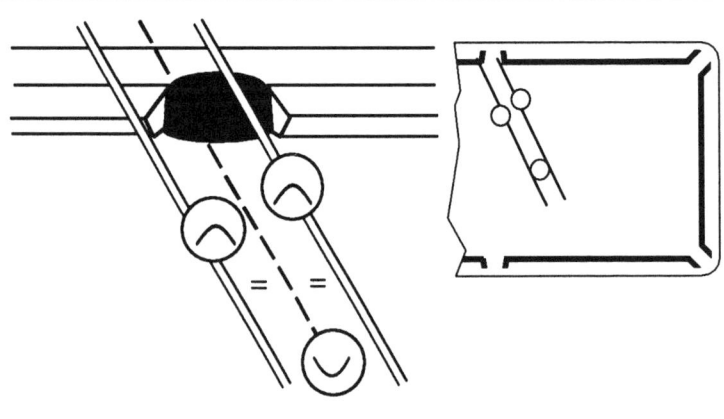

34

-TO EVERY TABLE
THE SHARPER THE ANGLE BECOMES

PIPER NOTE ♪ EXTRA...EXTRA...The tunnel gets smaller the faster you toss the Cue Stick! Yes...always!

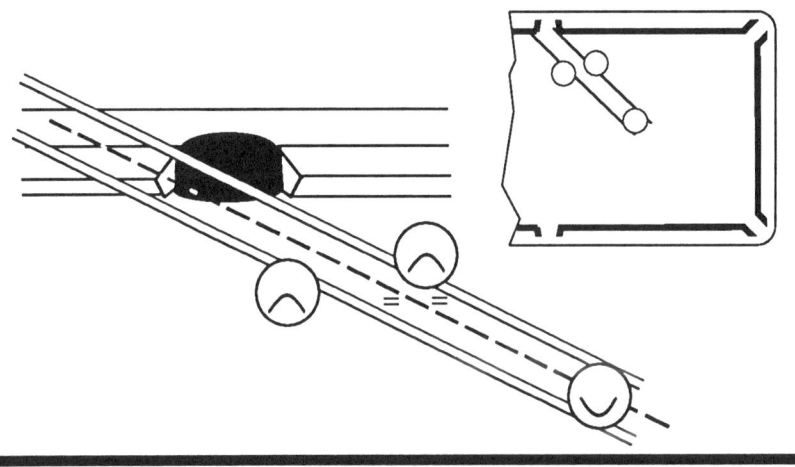

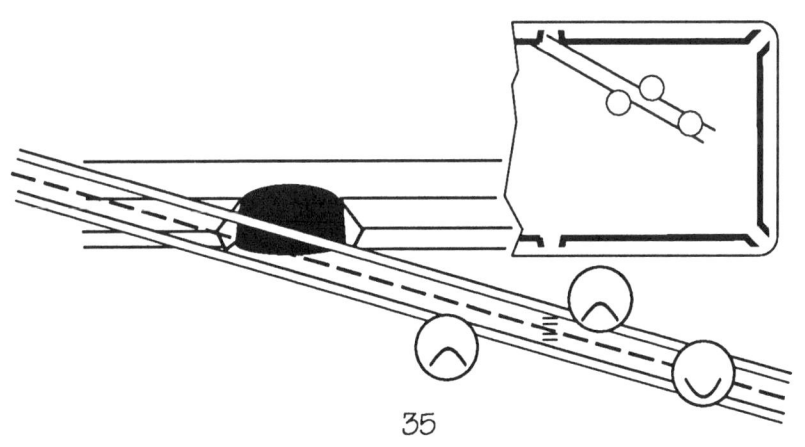

ALL THINGS BEING EQUAL

HERE IS SOME EQUAL TIME FOR THE STRIPED BALLS

MEET THE RACK-SPECIAL

ELEVEN BALL

My name is
EEK*WAL
I am for Equality.

PIPER
NOTE

THE ELEVEN BALL TURNED SIDE-WAYS IS AN EQUAL SIGN!

I AM A RED STRIPED BALL. I AM ROUND JUST LIKE A SOLID BALL. MY JOB IS TO POINT OUT ALL OF THE EQUALS IN POOL. HERE IS ONE NOW--

EACH SIDE OF THE CENTER LINE OF THE TUNNEL OF SMILES IS CALLED THE ERROR MARGIN. THEY ARE EQUAL SO IF YOU AIM FOR THE CENTER IT IS HARDER TO MISS..

HERE IS ANOTHER EQUAL

BALANCE YOUR WEIGHT ON YOUR OWN TWO FEET

RIGHTIES

LEFTIES

CUE STICK

CUE STICK

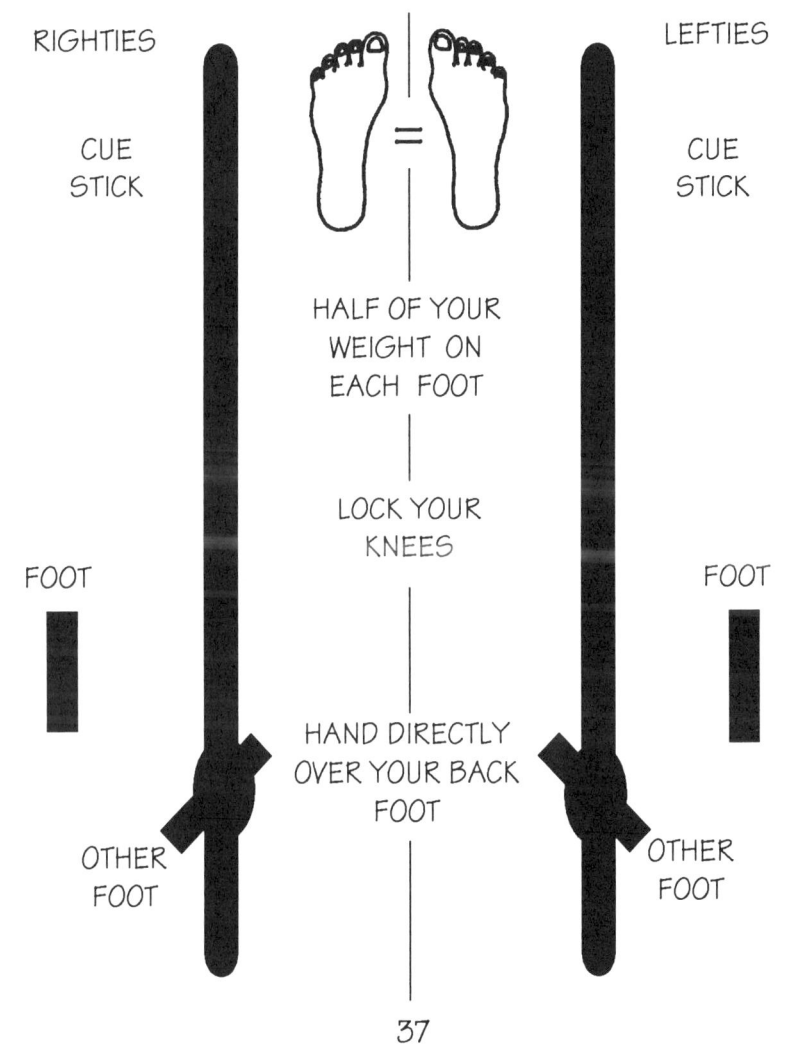

=

HALF OF YOUR WEIGHT ON EACH FOOT

LOCK YOUR KNEES

FOOT

FOOT

HAND DIRECTLY OVER YOUR BACK FOOT

OTHER FOOT

OTHER FOOT

KEEP YOUR CUE LEVEL!

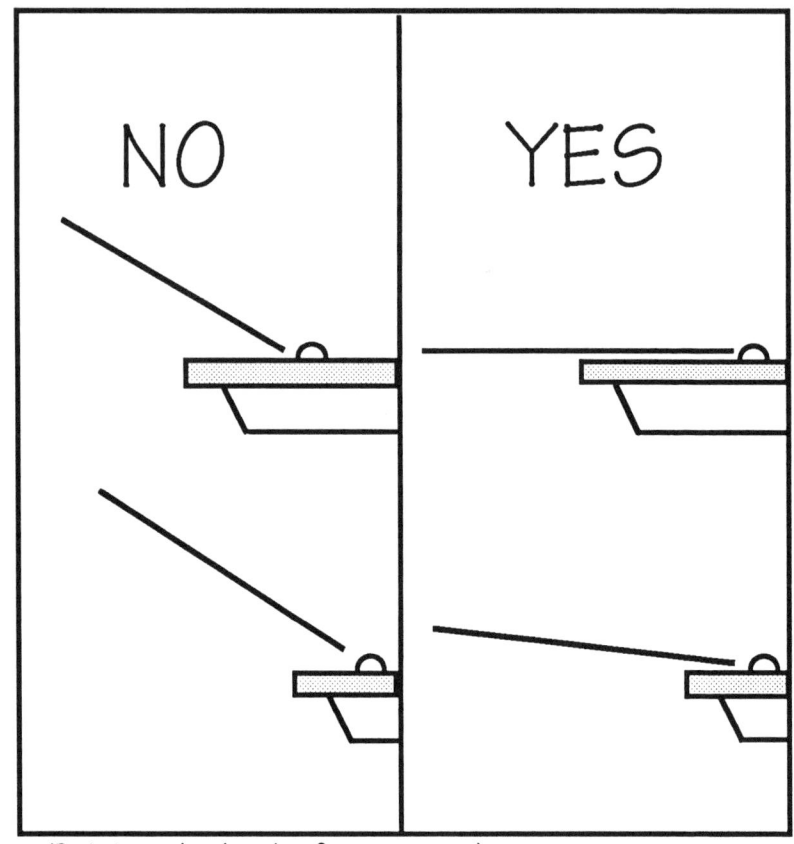

Raising the back of your cue _decreases_ accuracy because the Cue Ball "squirts" off the cloth -- that is very _unpredictable_. There is a raised stick shot called Massé. However, it should never be used unless the owner of the table says it is all right. Massé shots always harm the cloth, sometimes only a little, sometimes a lot.

TWELVE POINT TOSS CHECKUP

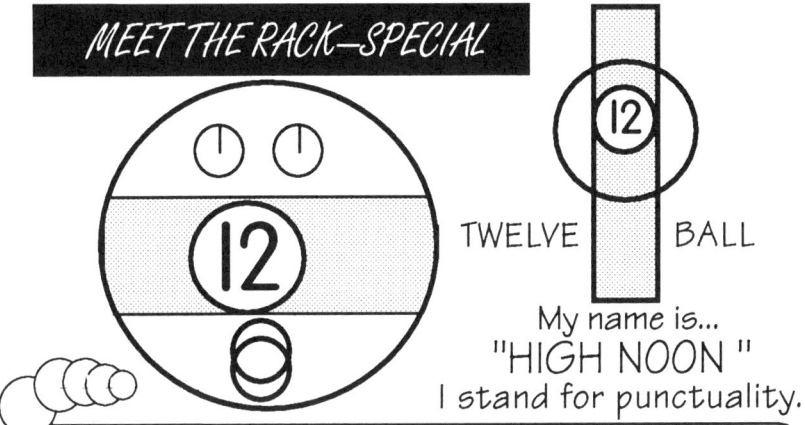

MEET THE RACK–SPECIAL

TWELVE BALL

My name is...
"HIGH NOON"
I stand for punctuality.

When you see me on the table remember these twelve points. 1.. Hold the Cue Stick firmly, not too tight. 2. Rest the Cue Stick in the V made by your open bridge. It should not come off the bridge after you toss. 3. Toss straight and on line. 4. Use a pendulum swing. 5. The backswing should be straight. 6. The distance of follow through equal to backswing. Freeze for a second before getting up. 7. Your stance should be balanced equally on your own two feet 8. Your head should be about six inches over the Cue Stick. 9. Your bridge arm should be straight or almost. 10. Keep your Cue Stick as level as possible. 11. Chalk your Cue Tip before every toss. 12. Think of slow motion just before you toss and think positively.

GAME NUMBER THREE
POCKET SHOOTING

HERE IS SOME MORE
POCKET SHOOTING.
THE SIDE POCKETS ARE
A LITTLE TRICKY!

Out of

A. *Put Rocky on the spot* --the footspot. Play the Cue Ball into each of the six pockets until you have made each pocket 7 out of 10 times.

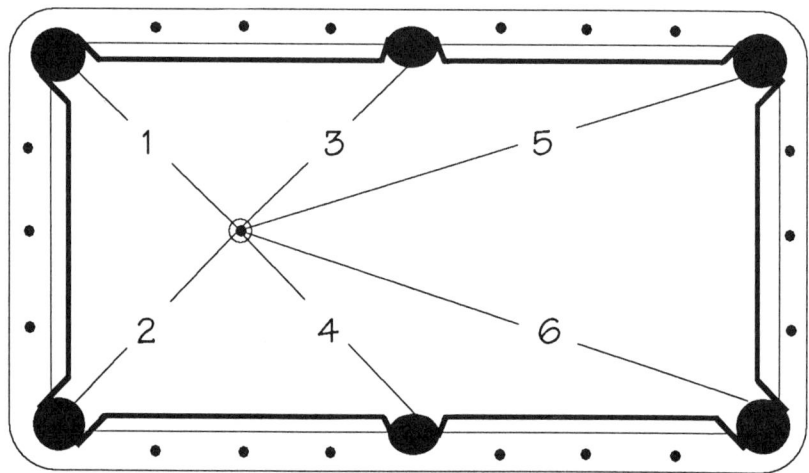

SUMMARY

I enjoy my time in the Land of Pool. I concentrate and when it is time to play I use what I have learned. That is why they call me "Q Time". Remember: The Tunnel of Smiles gets smaller as the angle gets thinner. The softer you toss the bigger the pockets. For now, aim for the center of the tunnel where the error margin is equal. Always keep your Cue Stick as level as possible.

PIPER NOTE

Decide what speed of toss you will use before you get into your stance. Use just the right speed to pocket the ball, for now. Later in the book you will use different speeds to set up an easy next play.

"EDDY CUT" OFFERS SHOTS ON ETIQUETTE

1. It is not cool to talk while your friend is getting ready to play. 2. It is not cool to chalk your Cue Stick loudly. 3. If a person at the table next to you is getting ready to play--wait till they are finished if you need the same space.

CHAPTER 4

THE POOL TROUBLESHOOTER

WHY DO I MISS SOMETIMES?

"I"

PIPER NOTE

WHEN YOU MISS ASK YOURSELF, "SELF, WAS THE <u>MISS</u> TOO FAR TO THE <u>LEFT OR RIGHT</u> OF THE POCKET?"

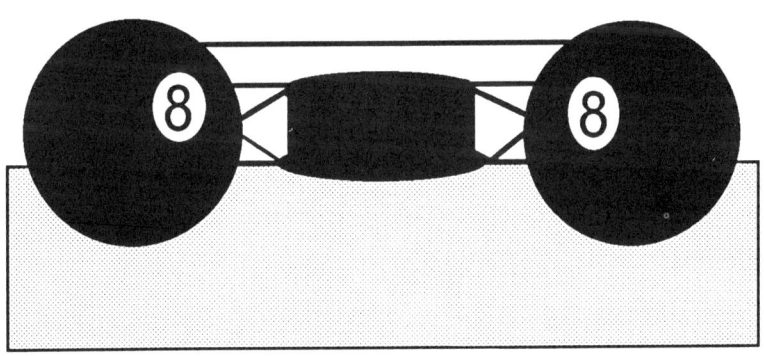

'TWAS a good thing to know--why I missed.

'TWAS a good thing to remember

T is for Toss: Did You Toss on Line?

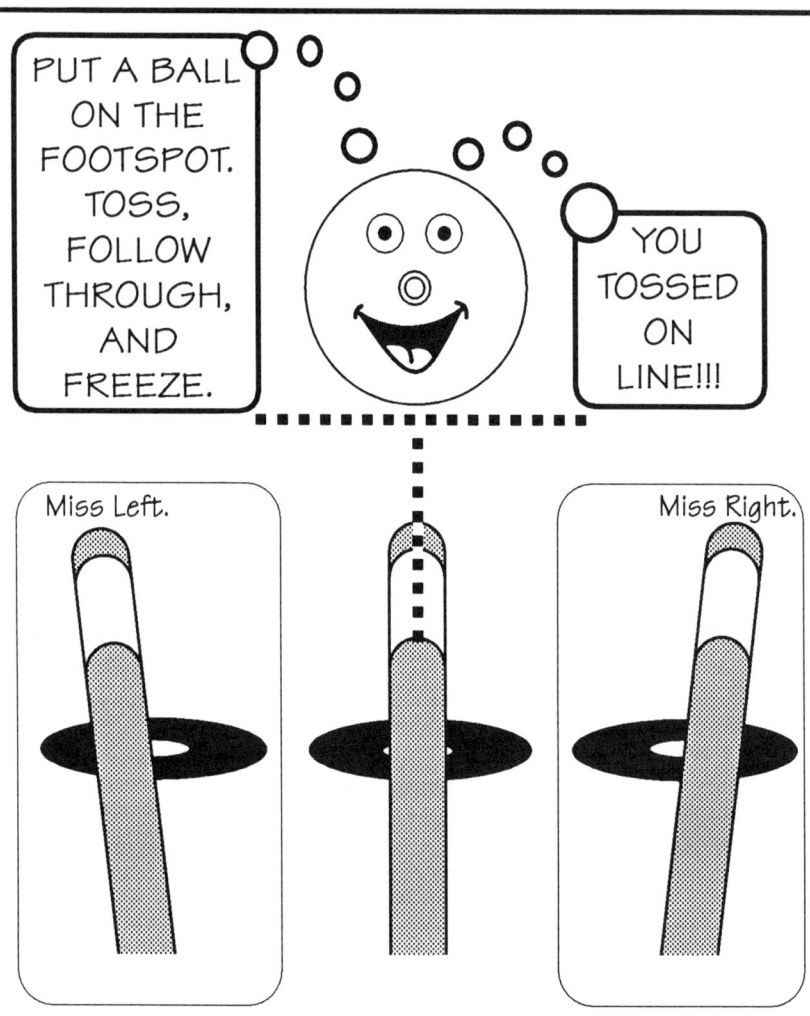

PUT A BALL ON THE FOOTSPOT. TOSS, FOLLOW THROUGH, AND FREEZE.

YOU TOSSED ON LINE!!!

Miss Left.

Miss Right.

'TWAS a good thing to remember

W is for Where to contact the Cue Ball

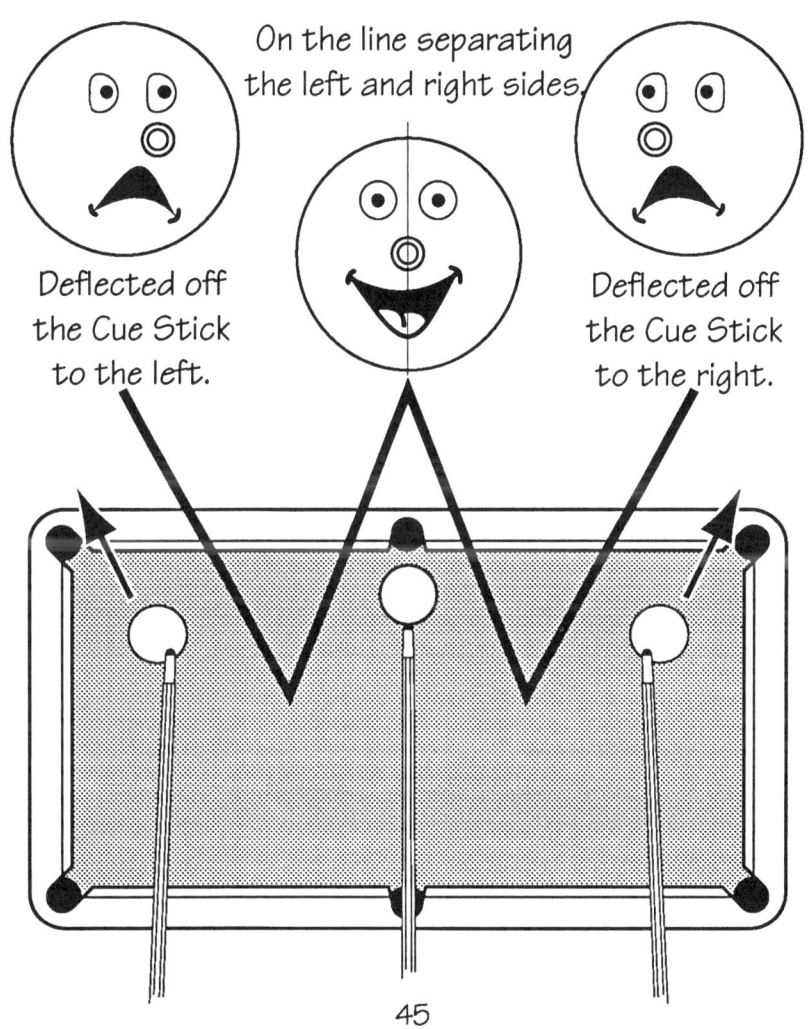

On the line separating the left and right sides.

Deflected off the Cue Stick to the left.

Deflected off the Cue Stick to the right.

'TW🅰S a good thing to remember

A is for Aim: Find the right line.

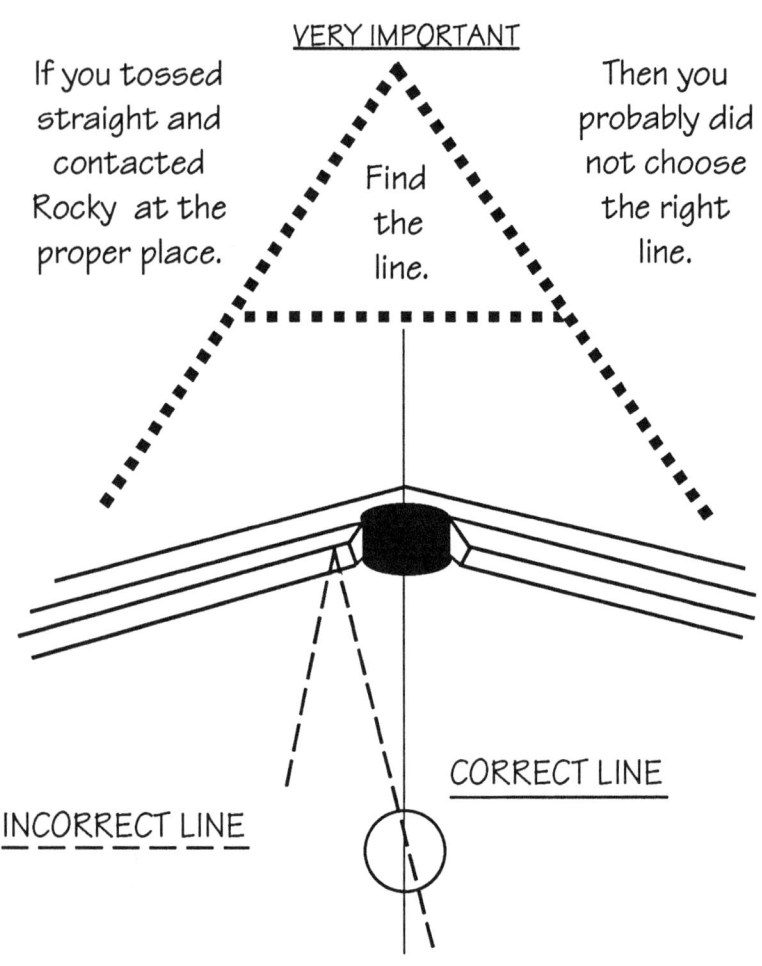

VERY IMPORTANT

If you tossed straight and contacted Rocky at the proper place.

Find the line.

Then you probably did not choose the right line.

INCORRECT LINE

CORRECT LINE

'TWA(S) a good thing to remember

S is for Speed control: Just enough

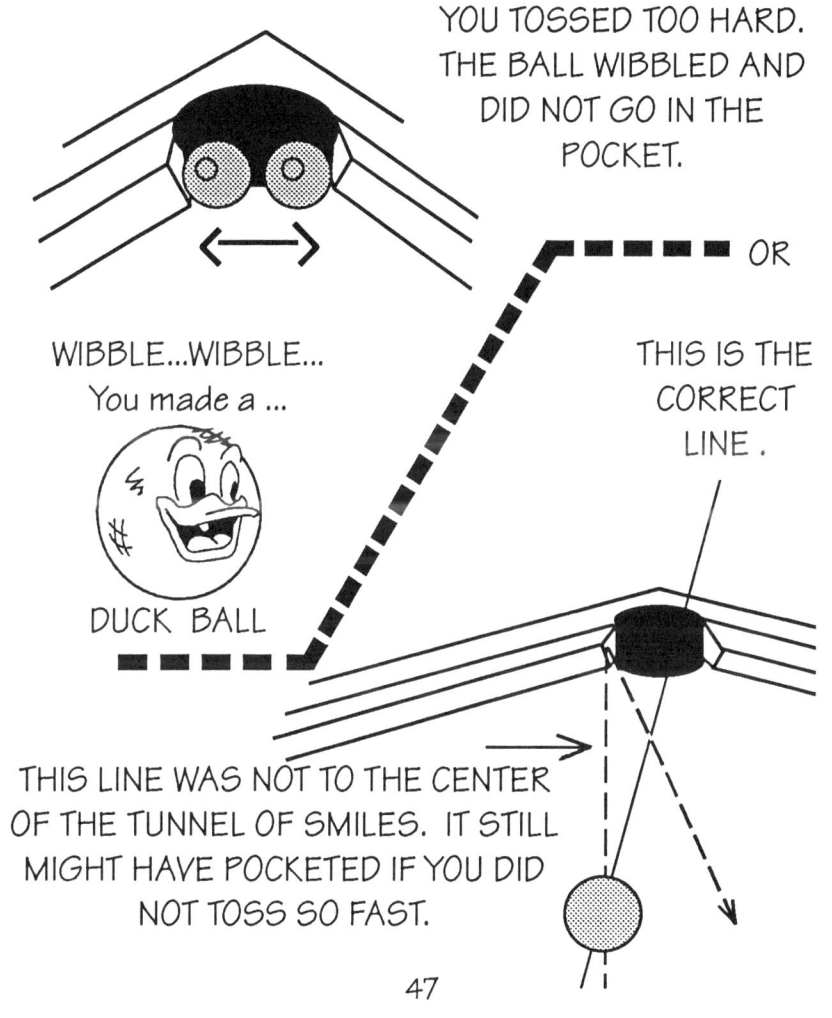

YOU TOSSED TOO HARD.
THE BALL WIBBLED AND
DID NOT GO IN THE
POCKET.

OR

WIBBLE...WIBBLE...
You made a ...

THIS IS THE
CORRECT
LINE .

DUCK BALL

THIS LINE WAS NOT TO THE CENTER
OF THE TUNNEL OF SMILES. IT STILL
MIGHT HAVE POCKETED IF YOU DID
NOT TOSS SO FAST.

POOL TROUBLESHOOTER

BAKER COOKS UP A 13 POINT CHECK-UP

MEET THE RACK—SPECIAL

Thirteen ⑬ Ball

My name is
BAKER
I am for generosity.

1. Check to see that your toss is staight and smooth.
2. Do not jump up after you toss--stay down.
3. Follow through the same distance as your backswing.
4. Your Cue Stick should not come off your bridge.
5. Make sure you contact the line between Rocky's left and right halves. 6. On which side of the pocket are you missing? Adjust your aim. 7. Keep your speed consistent. 8. Are you in the center of the Tunnel of Smiles? 9. Do not steer the Cue Stick--keep it on the line. 10. Do not bend your wrist --keep it solid. 11. If you miss--miss with confidence. 12. Is your practice toss straight? 13. (A Baker's Dozen is Thirteen not Twelve). Imagine the ball pocketing just before you toss.

IT IS IMPORTANT TO ALWAYS FOLLOW THE SAME CUE-UP STEPS BEFORE EACH PLAY!

TOSS SEQUENCE

STEP ONE: WHILE STANDING, CHOOSE THE POCKET CLOSEST TO THE BALL.	STEP TWO: IMAGINE A LINE TO THE CENTER OF THE POCKET (TUNNEL), AND PUT YOUR NOSE ON THE LINE.

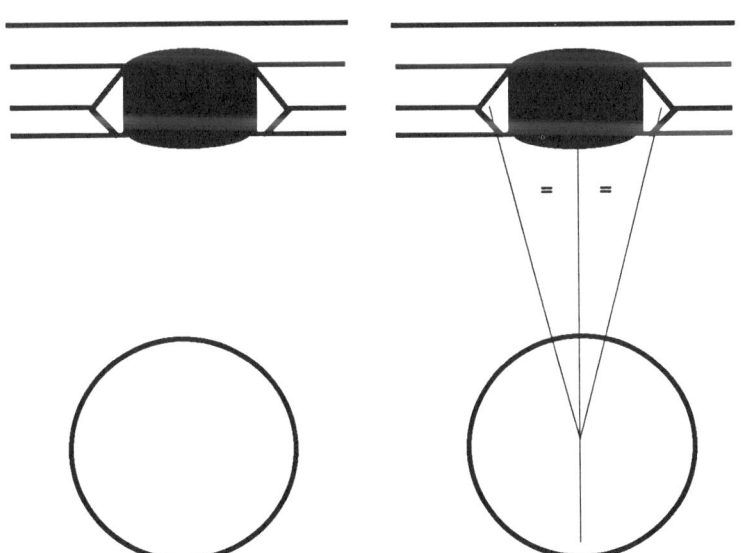

TOSS SEQUENCE

STEP THREE: SLOWLY PUT YOUR CUE STICK ON THE LINE, JUST ABOVE THE CUE BALL. KEEP IT ON THE LINE. BRING THE TIP OF YOUR CUE TO ONE HALF INCH FROM THE BALL--AND FREEZE.

STEP FOUR: IS THE CUE STICK ON LINE? IF NOT, GET UP-- NOW! REPEAT STEPS 1, 2 AND 3. DO NOT ADJUST YOUR AIM WHILE YOU ARE DOWN ON THE TABLE. IT IS TOO EASY TO MISS THAT WAY!

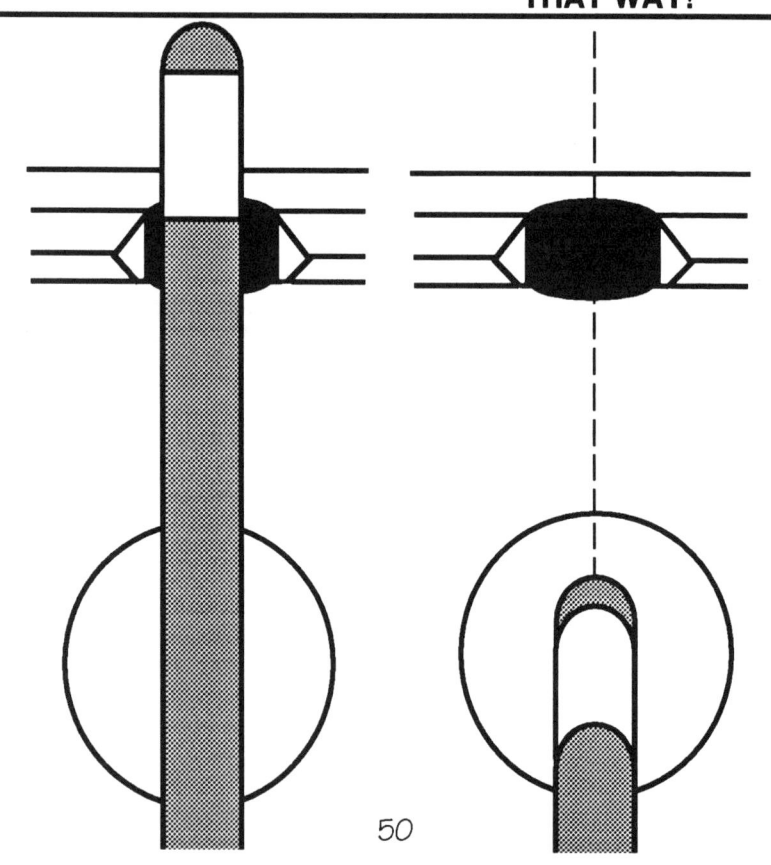

50

TOSS SEQUENCE

STEP FIVE: TAKE ONE, MAYBE TWO, PRACTICE TOSSES. IS THE TOSS STRAIGHT? ARE YOU GOING TO CONTACT THE PROPER POINT ON THE CUE BALL? IF IT DOES NOT FEEL RIGHT -- GET UP AND START OVER!

STEP SIX: IF IT FEELS RIGHT -- IMAGINE THE BALL POCKETING AND TOSS THE CUE STICK STRAIGHT. DID YOU ENTER THE POCKET AT THE CENTER LINE OF THE TUNNEL?

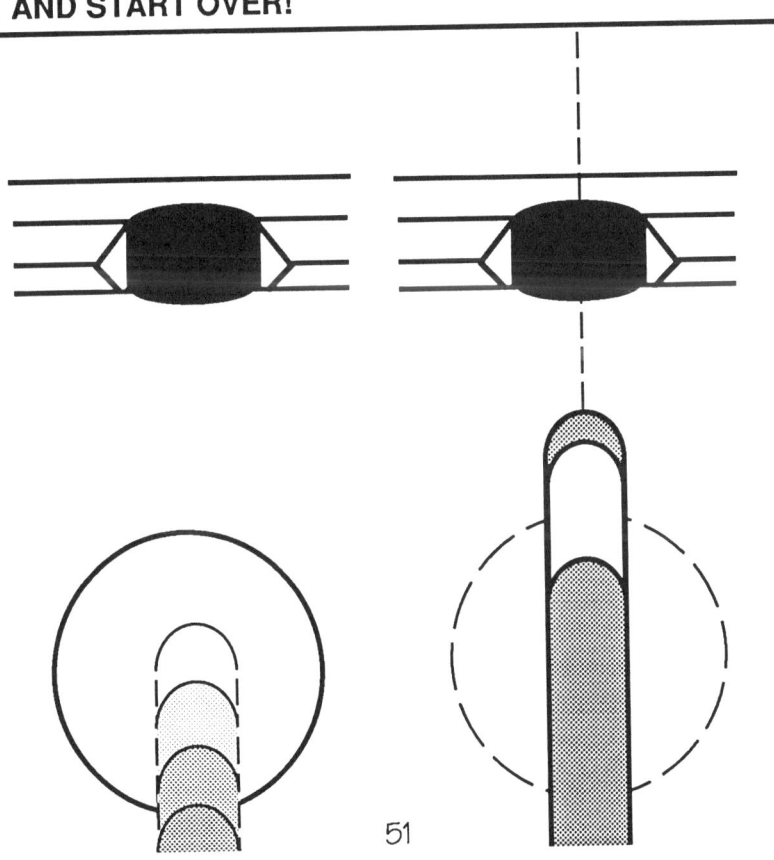

IF YOU ARE STILL HAVING PROBLEMS WITH AIM, YOU MIGHT WANT TO KNOW WHICH OF YOUR EYES IS DOMINANT. IT MIGHT BE HOW YOU SEE TO AIM.

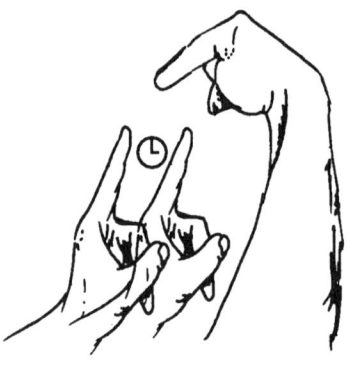

This is an experiment.

1. Look at a wallclock or other wall object.

2. Hold your left hand index finger up. If you keep your eyes on the clock you should see two fingers.

3. Center the two fingers around the clock.

4. With your right hand index finger (its left image--yes there are two of them, too), try and touch the left finger image.

5. Now try to touch the finger image on the right.

PIPER NOTE If you touched them both, your eyes are probably equally strong. If you touched only the *left--you are right eye dominant.* If you touched only the *right-- you are left eye dominant.* You may want to try putting your **dominant eye directly over the Cue Stick when aiming.** Try it and see if it is better.

BONUS AIMING SYSTEM: 'TWAS A GOOD ONE

GREY ZONE

Aiming is tricky.

If you look at the Pocket you see two Cue Sticks. If you look at the Cue Stick you see two Pockets.

PRETEND THAT THE CUE STICK IS YOUR LEFT HAND INDEX FINGER -- FROM THE LAST EXAMPLE-- AND THE BALL IS THE CLOCK. NOW YOU CAN SEE TWO STICKS INSTEAD OF TWO FINGERS.

FIND THE LINE FROM THE BALL TO THE CENTER OF THE TUNNEL OF SMILES. CENTER THAT LINE IN THE AREA BETWEEN THE TWO STICKS. THIS IS CALLED THE GREY ZONE.

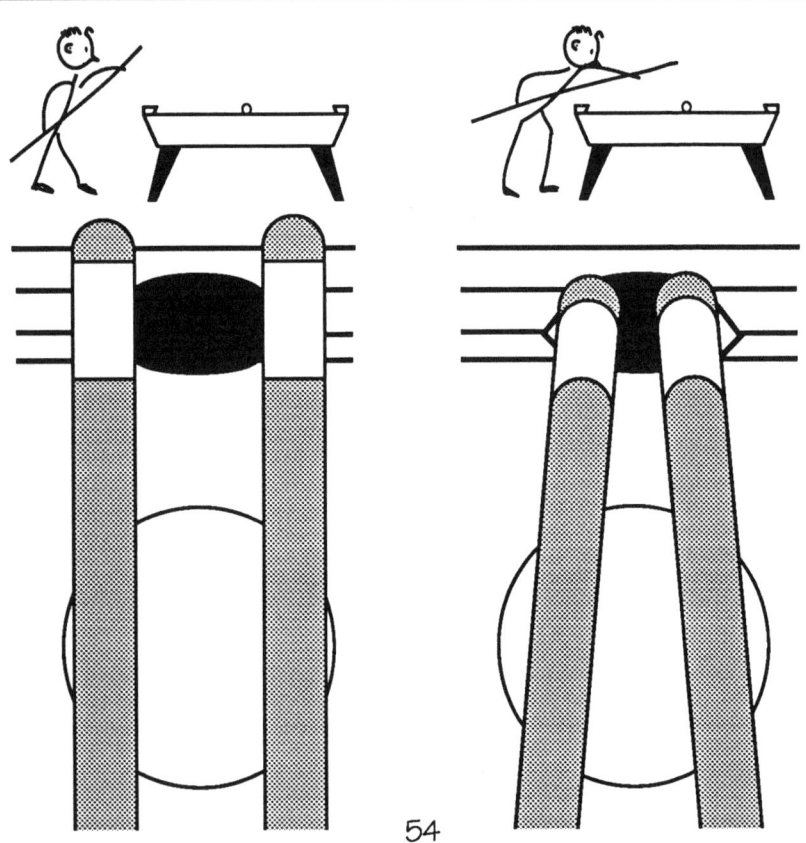

BRING THE CUE STICK DOWN AND BACK SLOWLY UNTIL IT ARRIVES AT A POINT ONE HALF INCH BEHIND THE CUE BALL AND ON THE LINE THAT SEPARATES ROCKY'S LEFT AND RIGHT HALVES.

MAKE SURE YOU ARE AIMING FOR A NATURALLY ROLLING BALL. YOU HAVE AIMED! IF YOUR PRACTICE TOSS(ES) ARE STRAIGHT THEN TOSS! YOU HAVE ENTERED THE GREY ZONE.

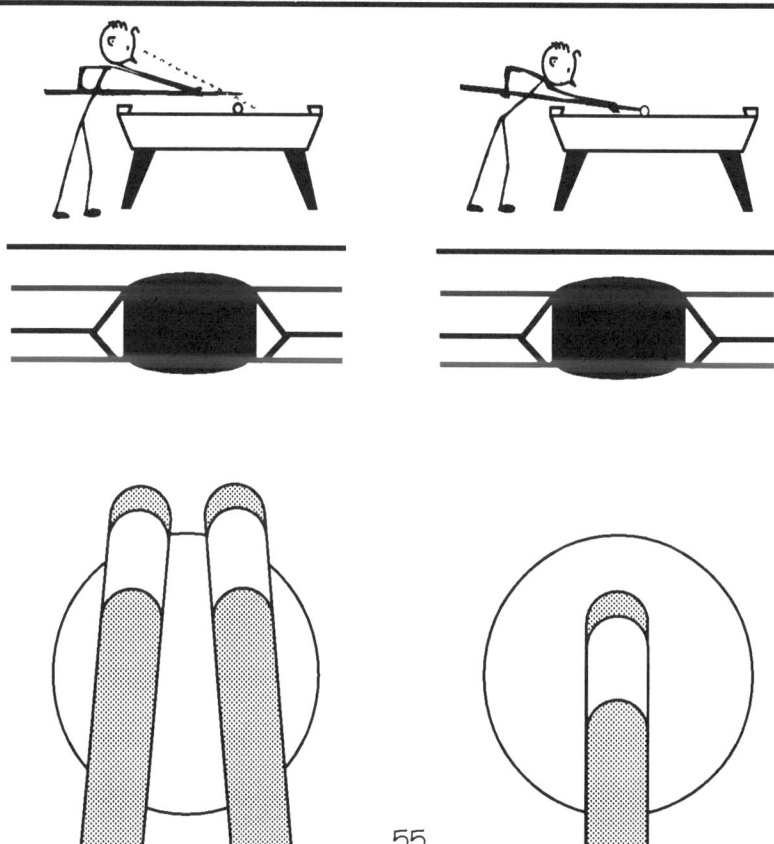

55

GREY ZONE II

If the ball is not entering the center of the pocket
(tunnel); when aiming, try putting the aim line a little to
the left of center in the Grey Zone-
-if your right eye is stronger.

Still cue up on the line that separates Rocky's left and right halves.

If your left eye is stronger, try putting the aim line
a little to the right of center in the Grey Zone.

GREY ZONE III

If your right eye is stronger, try putting the left image of
the Cue Stick directly on the aim line.

If your left eye is stronger try putting the right image of
the Cue Stick directly on the aim line.

 PIPER NOTE **Everyone is different. Find the system
that works for you. After you decide on
one, with practice it will become
second nature.
The Zone will be with you!**

SUMMARY

I only see one image of the Cue Ball and the pocket because I only see through one eye -
- I put the Cue Stick directly on the line. I still play great pool because I figure out why I miss and make corrections the next time up to the table. 'TWAS a good thing to remember: Toss on line: Where to contact Rocky: Aim for the center of the Tunnel of Smiles: Speed enough to pocket the ball. I don't have a decision to make on how to deal with putting my Cue Stick on the line--but you do. Try all the systems and stick (ha...ha...) with the best one.

PIPER
NOTE

The only thing you control in the Land of Pool is the Cue Stick. The Cue Stick controls the Cue Ball. The Cue Ball controls the rest. So learn how to handle a Cue Stick and you will play great Pool.

"EDDY CUT" OFFERS SHOTS ON ETIQUETTE

Sitting or leaning on the table can do great harm. It puts too much stress on the slates. Tables usually have three pieces of slate that are carefully fitted together. These seams may POP if you stress them and it won't play smooth anymore.

IT FEELS GOOD TO BE TOLD THAT YOU DID WELL...
YOU'LL FIND OUT, TOO!

CHAPTER

FIRST MEET ONE OF...
THE GREAT CONCEPT BALLS IN POOL ...

OBJECT
BALL
AND HIS
PET
SPOT

THE OBJECT BALL IS THE FIRST BALL YOU WANT TO CONTACT WITH THE CUE BALL.

SPOT IS INVISIBLE BUT THE FOLLOWING PAGE HAS THE TRICK TO LOCATE HIM.

THE IMAGINARY ROCKY

THE KEY TO AIMING PROPERLY

A MAGNIFICENT CONCEPT BALL

**WHEN SPOT AND THE OBJECT BALL LINE
UP ON THE CENTER OF THE TUNNEL OF
SMILES--IMAGINE ROCKY ON SPOT.
NOW ALL THREE OF THEM ARE LINED UP
FOR A SUCCESSFUL PLAY.**

THE NOT- SO IMAGINARY ROCKY

IS WHERE YOU PUT ROCKY TO START PLAYING

CRAZY EIGHTBALL: PART ONE

A FROZEN COMBINATION OR COMBO.

**THIS IS THE GAME THAT WILL TEACH YOU
HOW TO AIM WELL. PUT ROCKY RIGHT
ON SPOT!   ROCKY SHOULD BE
FROZEN (TOUCHING) TO THE OBJECT BALL
ON A DIRECT LINE TO THE CENTER OF THE
TUNNEL OF SMILES.**

CRAZY EIGHTBALL PART ONE
STRIPES AND SOLIDS

ONE PLAYER GETS THE TEAM STRIPES AND
THE OTHER PLAYER GETS THE TEAM SOLIDS.
WHOEVER POCKETS ALL OF THEIR TEAM MAY TRY TO
POCKET THE EIGHTSTER. THE PERSON THAT POCKETS
THE EIGHTSTER WINS!

I AM THE EIGHTSTER

I'M SPECIAL: THERE ARE
FIFTEEN BALLS IN A RACK.
SEVEN WITH LOWER
NUMBERS AND SEVEN
WITH HIGHER NUMBERS
AND ME.
I'M BLACK: NEITHER A
SOLID NOR A STRIPE.

SO THEY NAMED ALL THESE COOL GAMES
AFTER ME. WHOEVER POCKETS ME
AT THE RIGHT TIME WINS!!!

COMPOSITES NOT COMPOSITES
A MATHEMATICAL VERSION OF CRAZY EIGHTBALL

YOU WILL HAVE TO KNOW THE PRIME NUMBERS AND
COMPOSITE NUMBERS UNDER SIXTEEN TO PLAY THIS GAME.
NOT COMPOSITES WITH ONLY ONE EXCEPTION ARE PRIME
NUMBERS-- WHICH ARE ONLY DIVISIBLE BY THEMSELVES
OR ONE. WHOEVER POCKETS THE EIGHTSTER AFTER
POCKETING THEIR TEAM, WINS!
CAN YOU NAME THE TEAMS ?

ANSWER: SEE PAGE 63

TEAM STRIPES

Orange

YELLOW

RED

Green

Violet

PRIMARY COLORS:
YELLOW- 9 Nine T's
BLUE-   10 Aye O.
RED-   <u>11</u> Eek*wal
<u>Secondary colors:</u>
Violet-   12 High Noon
(made from red and blue)
Orange- <u>13</u> Baker
(made from red and yellow)
Green -14 Forethought
(made of blue and yellow)
_____
Burgundy- 15 Biggie
(made from red, blue and black)

BLUE NOTE: Subtract eight for color partner.

TEAM SOLIDS

Orange

YELLOW

RED

Green

Violet

PRIMARY COLORS:
YELLOW- <u>1</u> Captain
NOT PRIME OR COMPOSITE   Squint
BLUE-   <u>2</u> True Blue
RED-   <u>3</u> Sidekick
<u>Secondary colors:</u>
Violet-   4   Blinky
Orange- <u>5</u>   Hi Five
Green-   6   Marshal
_____ Newton
Burgundy- <u>7</u> Plato

BLUENOTE: Not Composites are Underlined. 63

RULE: **BALL-IN-HAND EVERY TOSS**

PRETEND THE EIGHTSTER IS THE CUE BALL

Ball-in-Hand means you can put the Cue Ball or in this
case the Pretend Cue Ball (Eightster) anywhere you like
on the table. In Part One put the Pretend Cue Ball
on the line with the Object Ball and the
center of the Tunnel of Smiles.

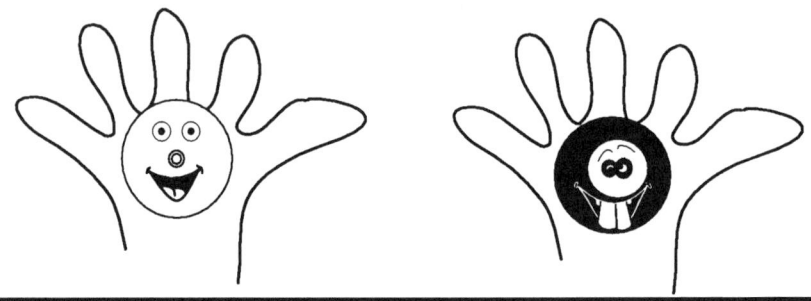

PUT THE CUE BALL ON SPOT.

PUT THE EIGHTSTER ONE FOOT AWAY ON LINE WITH THE CENTER OF THE TUNNEL OF SMILES.

"EDDY CUT " OFFERS SHOTS ON ETIQUETTE

If your friend gets Ball-in-Hand it is a
nice gesture to hand the ball
to your friend. Always wait till the
ball stops rolling, to pick it up.

LEARNING HOW TO FIND SPOT

1.. FIND THE
CENTER LINE OF THE TUNNEL TO THE POCKET

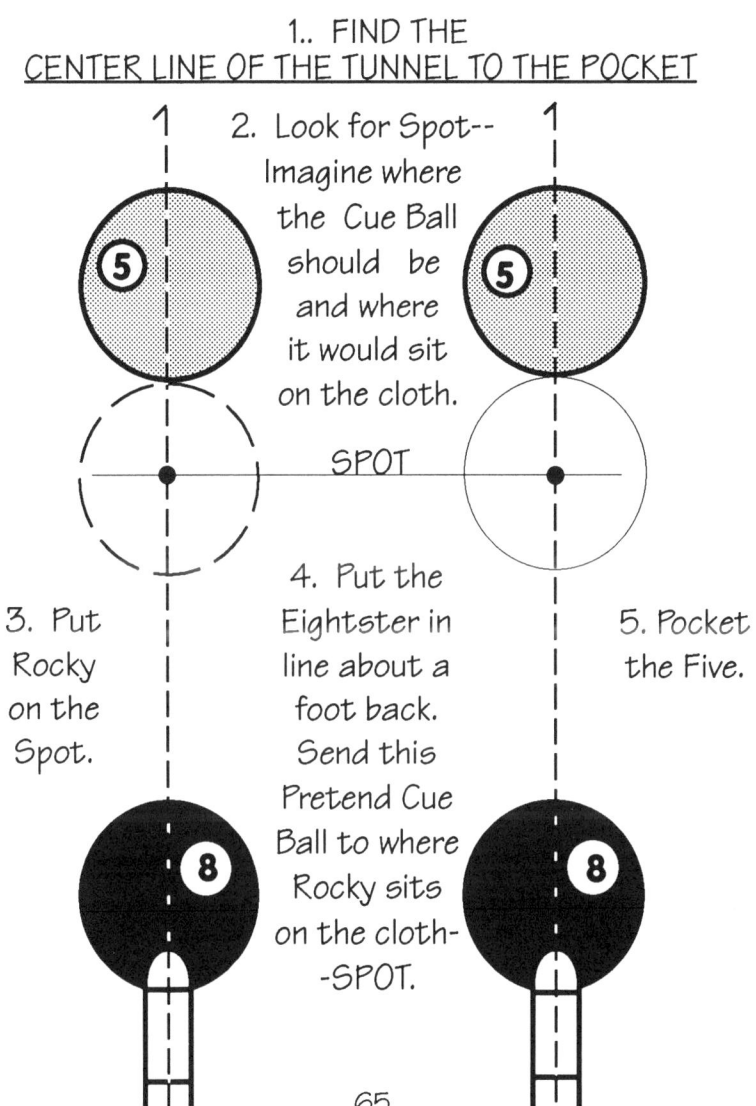

2. Look for Spot--
Imagine where
the Cue Ball
should be
and where
it would sit
on the cloth.

SPOT

3. Put
Rocky
on the
Spot.

4. Put the
Eightster in
line about a
foot back.
Send this
Pretend Cue
Ball to where
Rocky sits
on the cloth-
-SPOT.

5. Pocket
the Five.

HOW TO RACK FOR EIGHTBALL

1. All of the balls should be touching. This is called a tight or frozen rack. 2. The front ball should be directly on the footspot. If the longstring is marked on your table, the middle ball of the five balls in the last row should be sitting on the longstring. 3. The Eightster goes in the middle of the rack as shown. 4. A solid goes in one corner and a stripe in the other--it does not matter which corner. 5. It does not matter where the rest of the balls are placed in the rack.

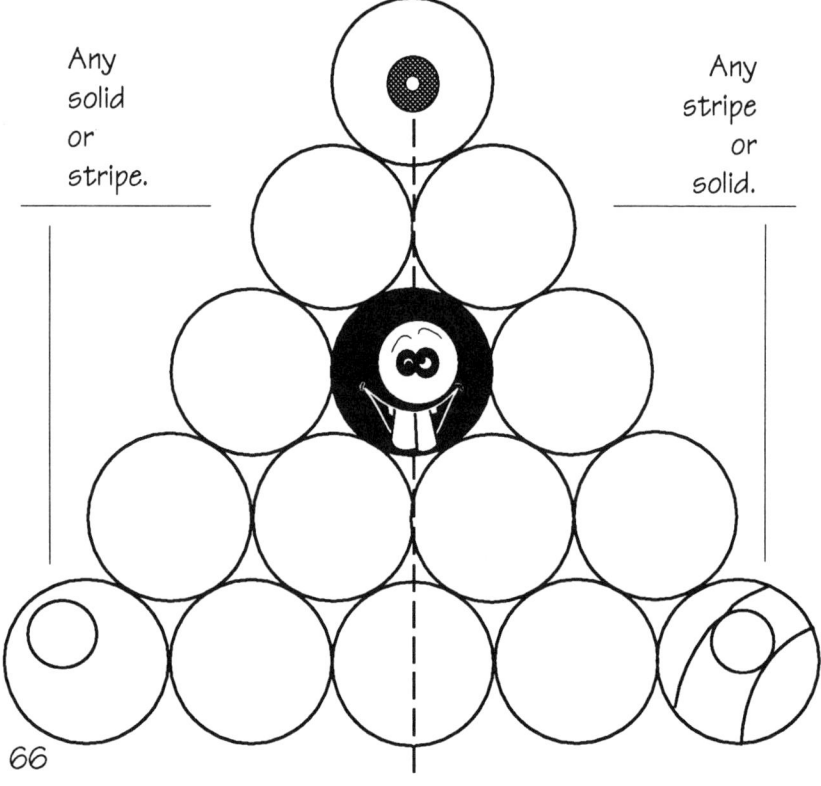

Any solid or stripe.

Any stripe or solid.

EEK*WAL'S SONG

Wel - come to the Land of Pool.

Come on in it's real - ly cool,

to make some friends in the Land of Pool.

The rack of balls is man - y hued

Each un - ique, but ev - en - ly qued,

for peace - ful - ly we play.

67

ANOTHER GREAT CONCEPT BALL

THIS IS THE CALLED BALL

AN INVITATION? TO THE SIDE?

In the great games of Crazy Eightball, you must call the ball and pocket into which you will put that ball. Example: Seven Ball in the Side Pocket.

Which side pocket you ask? The obvious one does not have to be specified. If, however, you mean to pocket the ball in the next closest pocket--that has to be called.

PIPER NOTE

A FUNNY THING ABOUT CALLED BALL AND POCKET IS THAT IT DOES NOT MATTER HOW THE BALL GETS THERE TO COUNT. THE BALL CAN GO AROUND THE TABLE THREE TIMES AND IF IT GOES IN THAT POCKET IT'S STILL GOOD.

ANOTHER GREAT CONCEPT BALL

THIS IS A TROUBLE BALL

SAVE ME!   DON'T SAVE ME!

A Trouble Ball is blocked to all pockets by the other team. It is very important to train yourself to count and keep track of every Trouble Ball on both teams.

If a Trouble Ball is your friend's then you do not want to move it out of its predicament (ask your parents), that is your friend's job. If you do move the ball it has a new name. You will learn that later (pg.111).

If the Trouble Ball is yours, then you need to find a way to get it out of trouble. Think about what that might be, we will talk more about that later, too.

PIPER NOTE DECISIONS...DECISIONS.   LOOK AT PAGE 71 AND SEE HOW THE CONCEPT OF A TROUBLE BALL HELPS TO PLAN YOUR STRATEGY.

CRAZY EIGHTBALL PART ONE

THE RULES

1. Break up the balls well or scatter them at random. The child plays first. If an adult and child are playing--let the adult break for now. There is a reference page on breaking on page 127 but it is advisable to leave it for later.

2. The table is open after the break. If the breaker sinks a ball on the break, it is their choice stripes or solids. If nothing is pocketed on the break it is the other person's choice. When the Called Ball is pocketed in the called pocket the teams are chosen.

3. It is still your turn if you pocket the Called Ball in the called pocket. If you miss it is your friend's turn.

4. Once you have pocketed all your team you may try to pocket the Eightball. If you sink the Eightball in the called pocket you win.

5. No fouls are called in Part One.

70

STRIPES OR SOLIDS?

You broke up the rack and pocketed two stripes. It is still your choice-- teams are not decided until the first Called Ball is pocketed in the called pocket. Find every Trouble Ball, which team has more? Which team do you want?

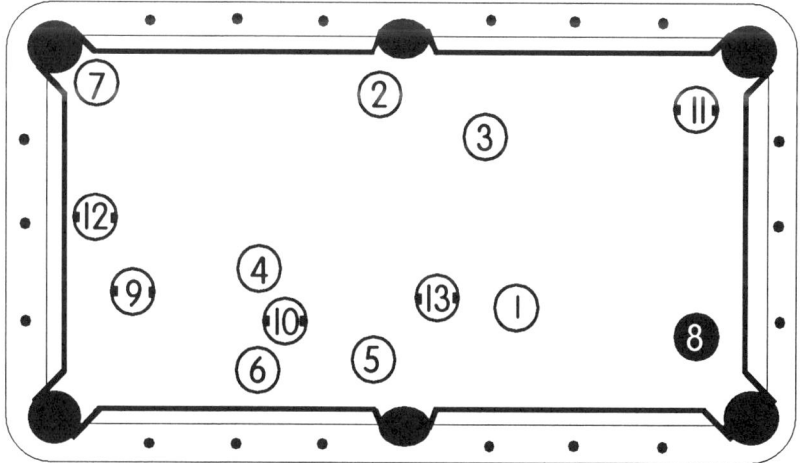

Answer is on the next page.

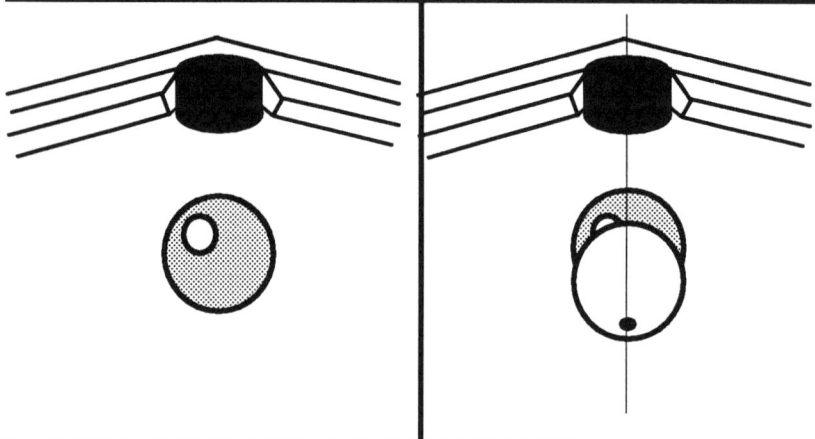

Find the pocket with the widest Tunnel of Smiles for the Object Ball. Find the center line. Now find the Object Ball's pet Spot.

Put Rocky on Spot, so the Object Ball and Rocky are touching or very close. Now you can see the Not-so Imaginary Rocky.

PIPER NOTE

ANSWER TO QUESTION ON PREVIOUS PAGE.
TAKE SOLIDS, STRIPES HAS TWO IN TROUBLE
(THE TEN AND THE TWELVE-ALTHOUGH IT IS
BLOCKED TO ITS POCKET BYA MEMBER OF ITS
OWN TEAM, IT STILL IS NOT EASY), **SOLIDS ZERO.**
EVEN THOUGH THERE ARE TWO LESS STRIPES ON
THE TABLE IT IS EASIER TO POCKET TEAM SOLIDS.

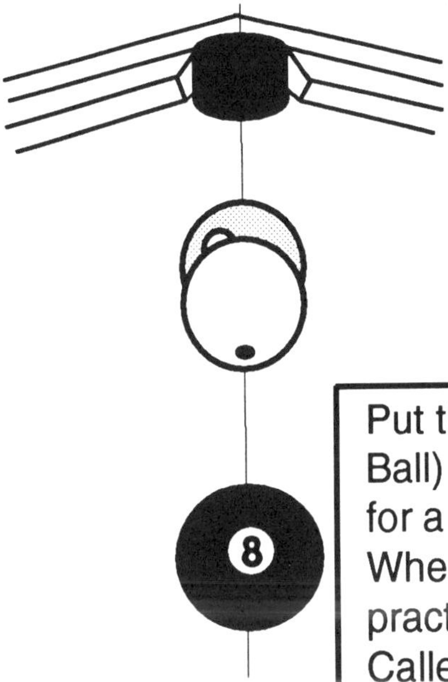

CORRECT

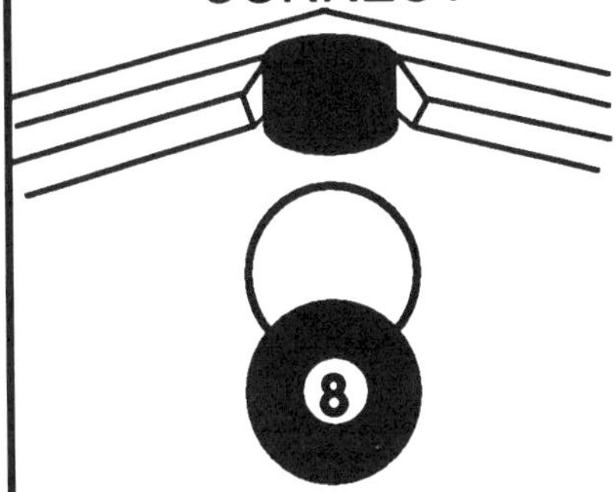

Put the Eightster (Pretend Cue Ball) on the same line. Set up for a natural rolling play. When you have a straight practice toss, imagine the Called Ball pocketing and toss the Cue Stick straight.

WRONG: EVEN IF YOU POCKETED THE BALL

You contacted the combo a little too far to the left.

You contacted the combo a little too far to the right.

HOW TO WIN--CRAZY EIGHTBALL #1

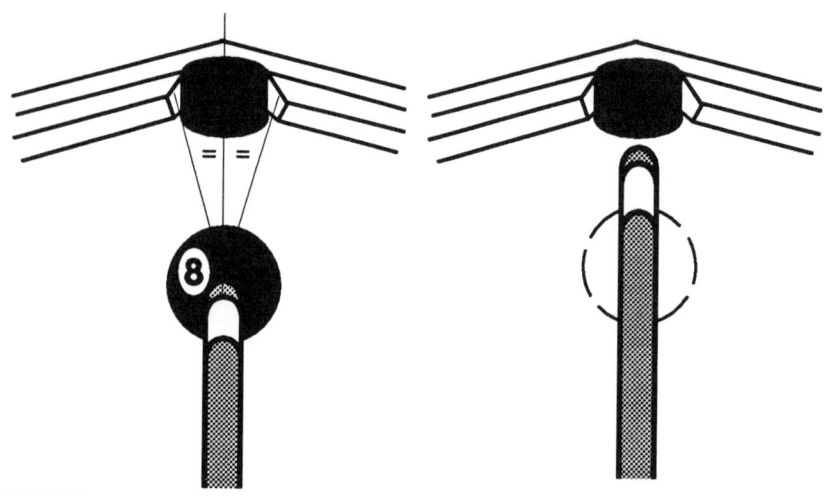

| After you have pocketed all of your team, you can play the Eightster directly into the pocket. If you miss it is your friend's turn, if your friend misses it is your turn. | You cannot move Rocky out of the way to play the Eightster. If Rocky blocks a pocket you must play the Eightster in a different pocket. When you sink the Eightster you can say... |

RACK 'EM, PLEASE!

SUMMARY

PIPER
NOTE

Some people think girls can not play pool. I learned all the basics and I show them! I play very well. Remember: Find Spot. The line Spot is on with the Object Ball should be the center line to the Tunnel of Smiles. The Called Ball in the called pocket make up a Called Shot-- Always call your shot unless it is obvious. Ball-in-Hand means you can put the Cue Ball anywhere on the table you want (or the Eightster in Part One). Look out for the Trouble Ball!

If you are using the Grey Zone aiming system, the line you use now is from the Cue Ball to Spot. For now you are pretending the Eightster is the Cue Ball but starting in the next chapter you will use Rocky.

"EDDY CUT" OFFERS SHOTS ON ETIQUETTE

Interfering with your friend's Cue Stick or team is not funny. Only babies do that. In a tournament you lose the game for it. BONUS: After racking hang the rack back under the table--if you leave it on the floor someone may trip over it.

the game of **EIGHTBALL**
Meet the Rack...

The Six is Team Player.

HEY KID...

"Obey the laws in the Land of Pool"

– Newton, Chief of the Billiard Police

LEARN

S K I D

My Name is...
MARSHAL NEWTON

IN THE LAND OF POOL-
-PHYSICS RULE

CHARTER

PART II

To Pocket your team, switch the Cue Ball and
the Eightball in the frozen combinations.

To Pocket the Eightball use the Cue Ball.

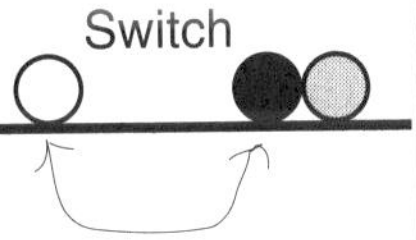

Switch

Now that you
know where
Spot is and
how to use the
Imaginary Ball
concept--
Switch to the
real Cue Ball.

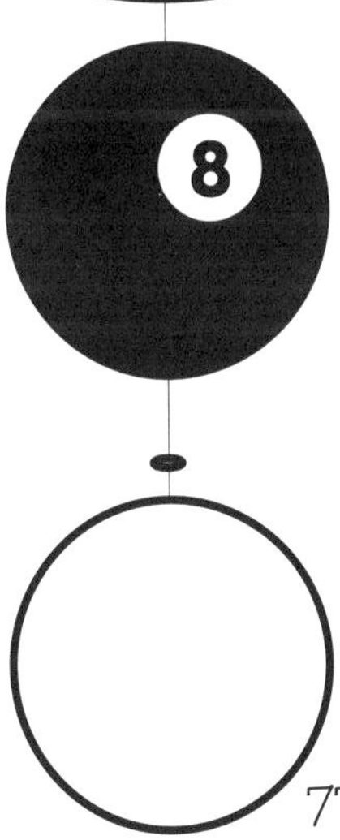

8

NEW ENDING

You have Cue
Ball-in-Hand.
Put Rocky on
the line
in front of
the Eightball
and
the pocket
and toss!

WHILE STANDING, PICK THE POCKET CLOSEST TO THE OBJECT BALL. IMAGINE A LINE FROM THE CENTER OF THE TUNNEL OF SMILES THROUGH THE BALL.

FIND WHERE THE IMAGINARY CUE BALL WOULD BE AT THE MOMENT OF CONTACT. FIND SPOT. PUT THE CUE BALL ON THE LINE A FOOT AWAY.

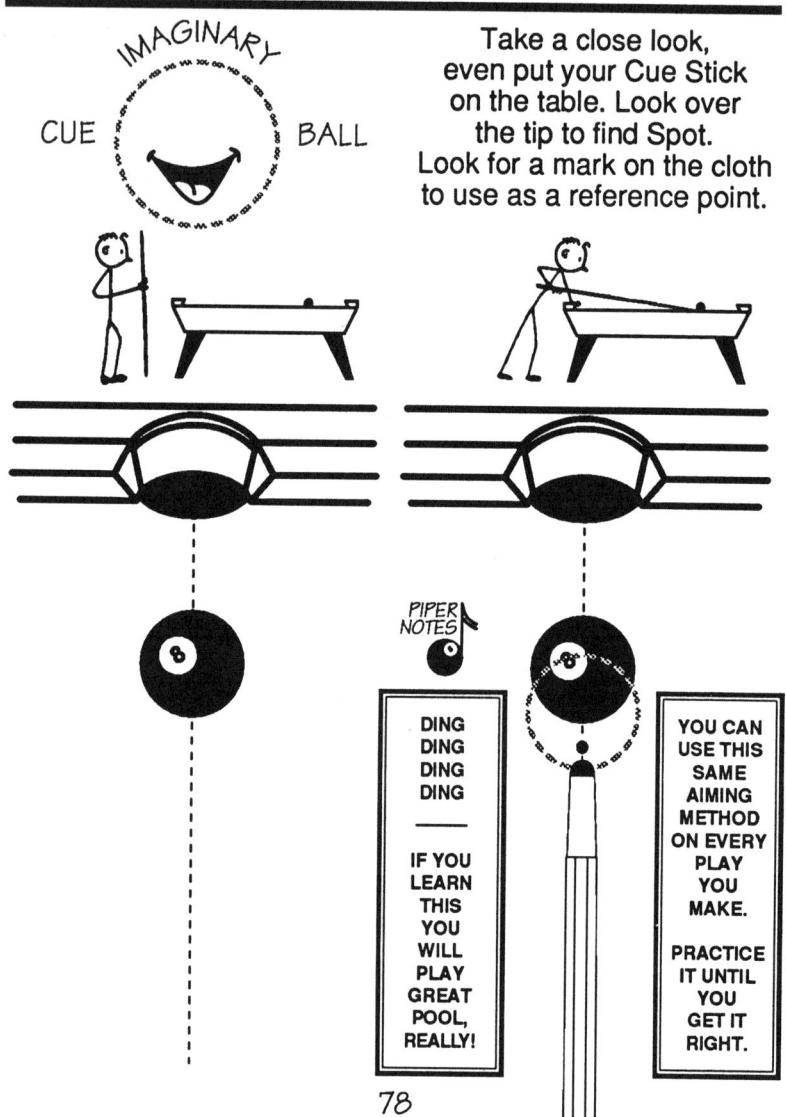

IMAGINARY

CUE BALL

Take a close look, even put your Cue Stick on the table. Look over the tip to find Spot. Look for a mark on the cloth to use as a reference point.

PIPER NOTES

DING
DING
DING
DING
—
IF YOU LEARN THIS YOU WILL PLAY GREAT POOL, REALLY!

YOU CAN USE THIS SAME AIMING METHOD ON EVERY PLAY YOU MAKE.

PRACTICE IT UNTIL YOU GET IT RIGHT.

PUT YOUR NOSE ON THE LINE
AND GET INTO YOUR STANCE.
BRING THE CUE DOWN
ON THE LINE.

YOU HAVE COMPLETED AIMING.
TEST YOUR TOSS
TO SEE IF IT IS STRAIGHT.

Don't take your eyes
off of the Spot.

Toss the Cue Stick
straight!

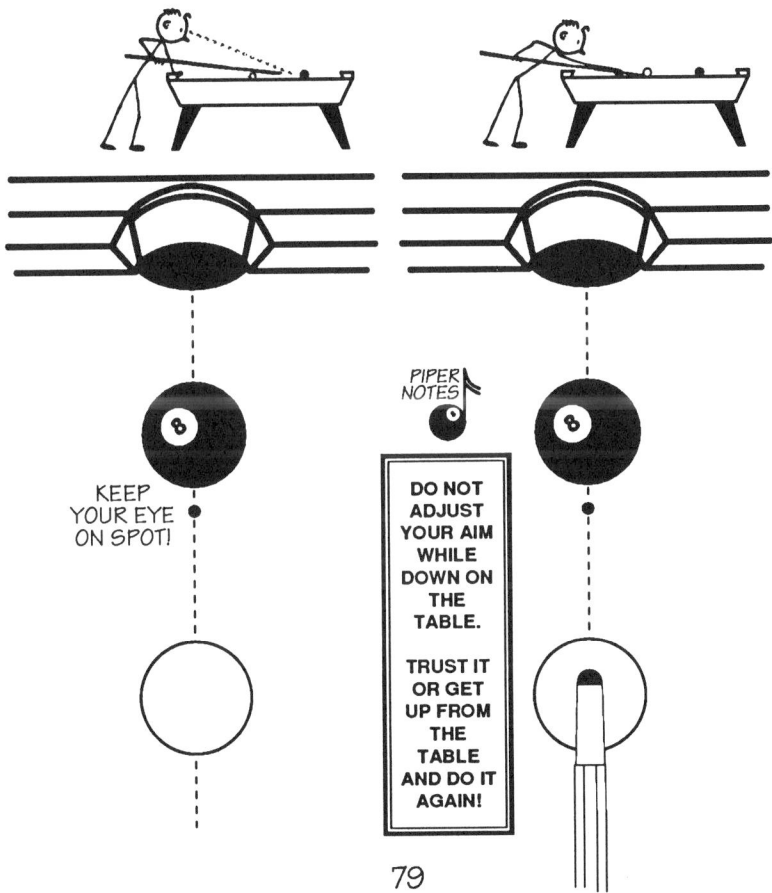

KEEP
YOUR EYE
ON SPOT!

PIPER NOTES

DO NOT
ADJUST
YOUR AIM
WHILE
DOWN ON
THE
TABLE.

TRUST IT
OR GET
UP FROM
THE
TABLE
AND DO IT
AGAIN!

WHAT DO YOU MEAN IT DOES NOT COUNT IF ROCKY POCKETS? RUN THAT BY ME AGAIN!

WHAT IS A SCRATCH?

YIKES....I NEVER ITCH.

PIPER NOTE

IT IS NOT GOOD TO POCKET THE CUE BALL. YOU LOSE YOUR TURN.

NEW RULE

IF YOU POCKET ROCKY-- ANY OF YOUR TEAM THAT WERE POCKETED ON THE PLAY COME BACK UP AND ARE PUT ON THE FOOTSPOT (OR LONGSTRING AS CLOSE TO THE FOOTSPOT AS POSSIBLE).

HOW DO I PREVENT
SCRATCHING ON A
STRAIGHT IN PLAY?

TWO WAYS TO AVOID A SCRATCH

1. TOSS VERY SOFTLY SO ROCKY DOES NOT MAKE IT
   TO THE POCKET BUT THE OBJECT BALL WILL.

2. PIN ROCKY'S NOSE LOWER ON HIS FACE.

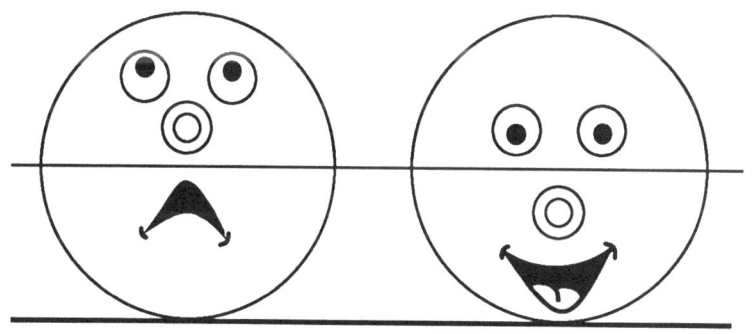

THERE IS A THIRD AND FOURTH WAY
LATER IN THE BOOK.

WHY WILL THIS PREVENT A SCRATCH?

ROCK SLIDE SLIM STOPS ON SPOT

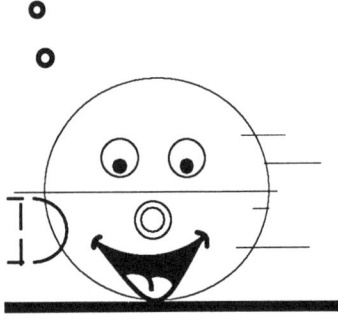

They call me Rock Slide Slim because I stop on Spot's place if I contact the Object Ball straight-on while sliding or skidding and I am not kidding.

What does SPOTS spell backwards?

I am out of here. Rocky transfers energy to me and I am gone.

STOPS

SIDE VIEW

82

BACKSPIN   SLIDE   R O L L

TOSS LOWER AND/OR FASTER TO MOVE
THE SKID/SLIDE ZONE FORWARD AND
MAKE IT LONGER.

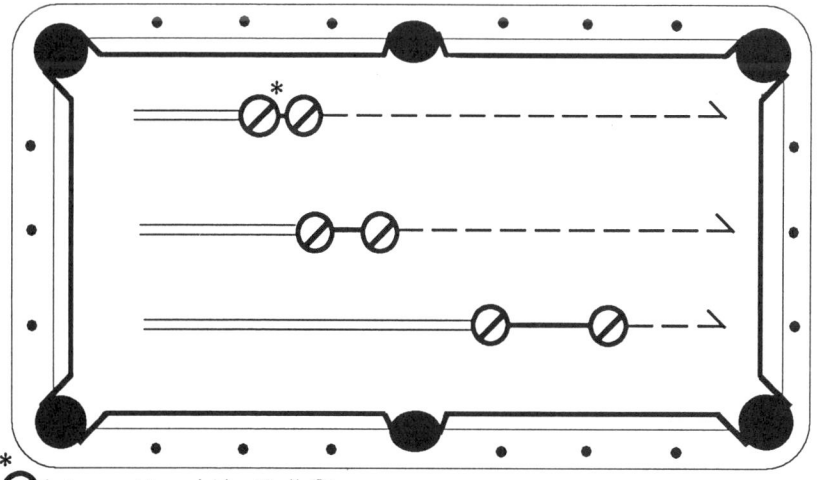

RAIL SH⬤TS

OBJECT BALL FROZEN ON THE RAIL

These take a lot of practice. You have to contact the cushion slightly before the Object Ball. You can do this by finding Spot and moving him back the thickness of a dime or two. A little extra speed of toss is good, too, so the Cue Ball sinks into the rail.

PIPER NOTE **Try different angles and distances to the pocket. Use the same speed each time. Then try it all again with different speeds.**

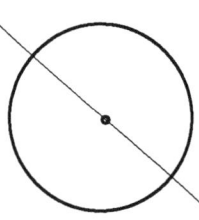

84

Everyone must pocket their team with
Cue Ball-in-Hand (No frozen combos).
The Eightball must be pocketed by a
HALF BALL play with Cue Ball-in-Hand.

WHAT IS A HALF BALL PLAY? IT IS WHERE THE LINE
OF AIM THROUGH SPOT RUNS THROUGH THE EDGE
OF THE OBJECT BALL. THEY ARE ALMOST AS EASY
TO AIM AT AS A STRAIGHT-IN PLAY. THERE ARE
TWO HALVES TO EVERY PLAY, TOO.

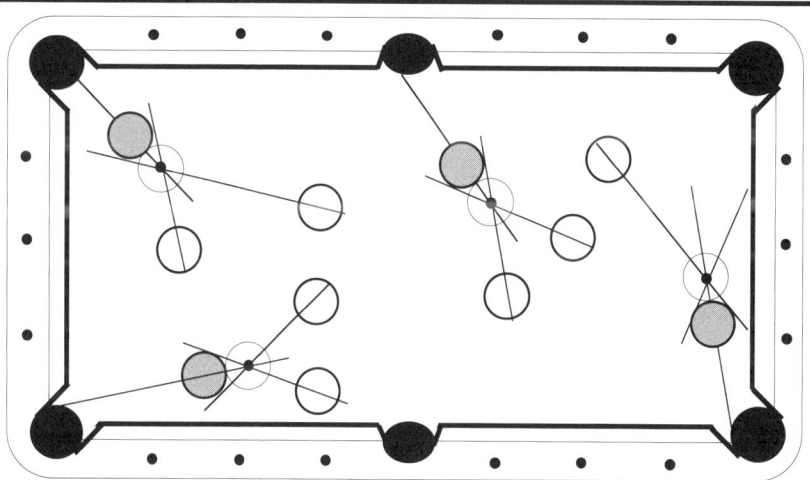

I'M NOT QUITE SURE I UNDERSTAND HOW TO
USE BALL-IN-HAND AND FIND THE EXACT
PLACE TO PUT IT TO GET A HALF BALL PLAY.

HOW TO SET UP-

FIND SPOT-- ON THE DIRECT LINE TO THE CENTER OF THE TUNNEL OF SMILES.

WALK YOUR NOSE TO THE POINT WHERE A LINE FROM IT THROUGH SPOT TOUCHES THE EDGE OF THE OBJECT BALL.

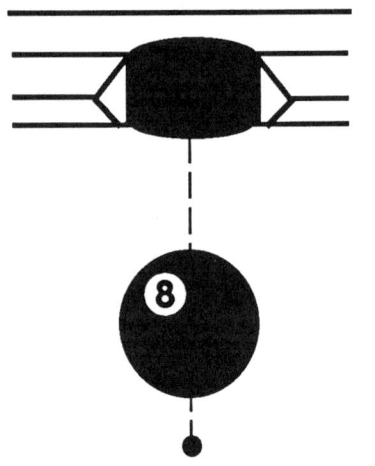

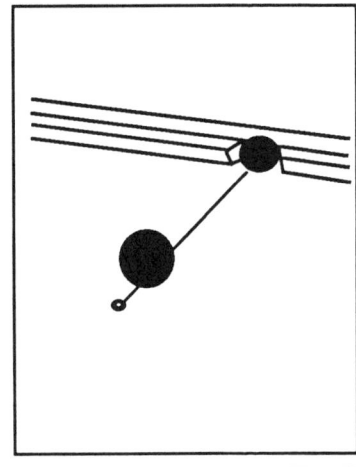

 PIPER NOTE A HALF BALL PLAY IS YOUR FIRST CUT SHOT. A CUT SHOT IS ANY PLAY THAT IS NOT STRAIGHT IN. A HALF BALL PLAY IS THE EASIEST CUT SHOT OF THEM ALL.

-A HALF BALL

PLACE
THE CUE
BALL ON
THAT
LINE.

TO WIN IN
PART III
HALVE
THE
EIGHTBALL!

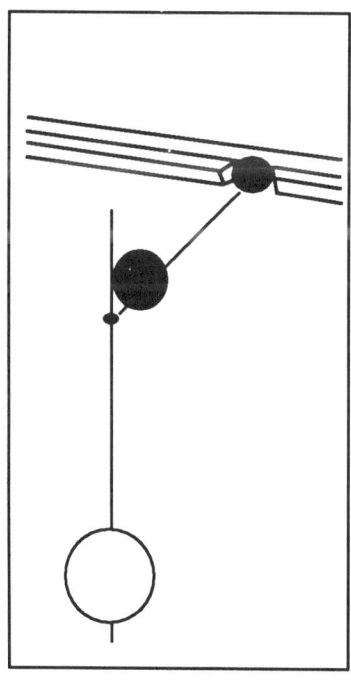

IF YOU MISS THE POCKET ON THE LEFT (FAR) SIDE- -YOU MAY BE LOOKING FOR SPOT TOO CLOSE TO THE EIGHT. IF YOU ARE SURE THAT YOU ARE SETTING UP THE PLAY CORRECTLY BUT ARE STILL MISSING ON THE FAR SIDE --SKIP AHEAD TO CHAPTER 7 AND COME BACK TO THIS. YOU HAVE STUMBLED ONTO THE BIGGEST SECRET IN POOL ALL BY YOURSELF!!

THE NAME OF THE GAME IS POSITION

To pocket your team you get
Ball-In-Grasp (Hand) every other play.
SO GRASP YOUR B-I-G OPPORTUNITY.
Use what you have learned to get POsition on
your next ball.

To pocket the Eightball you must play it where it and
the Cue Ball lie--**NO** Cue Ball-in-Hand.

STOP SHOTS--THE EASIEST POSITION PLAY

TWO BALL RUNS

PIPER NOTE

**START WITH CUE BALL-IN-HAND AND LOOK FOR
STOP SHOTS THAT GIVE YOU A GREAT NEXT PLAY.**

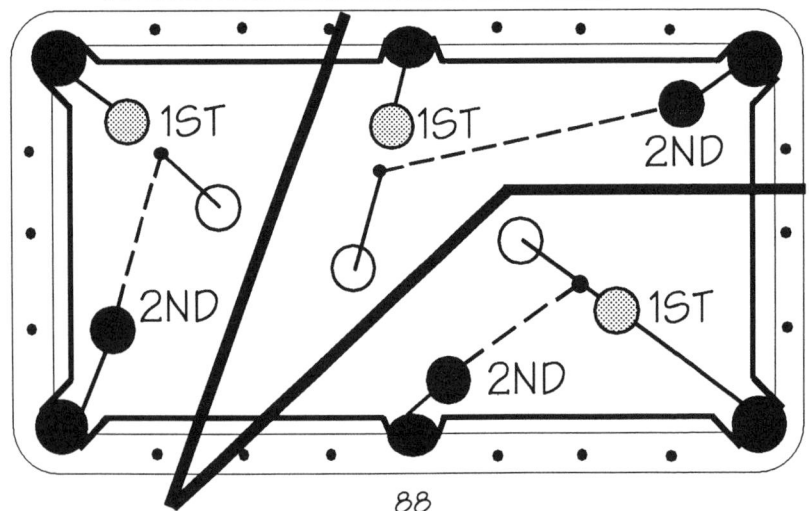

TWO BALL RUNS

STRAIGHT-IN FORWARD ROLLS

IT IS ALWAYS *GOOD* TO MOVE THE CUE BALL AS LITTLE AS POSSIBLE TO GET GOOD POSITION ON YOUR NEXT PLAY.

PIPER NOTE

GOING FORWARD (NATURAL ROLL) IS THE NEXT MOST RELIABLE WAY TO GET POSITION. REMEMBER, A BALL HAS GOT TO DO WHAT A BALL HAS GOT TO DO. DO NOT TOSS TOO FAST OR YOU WILL SCRATCH. A VERY SLIGHT ANGLE WILL PREVENT THE SCRATCH, TOO.

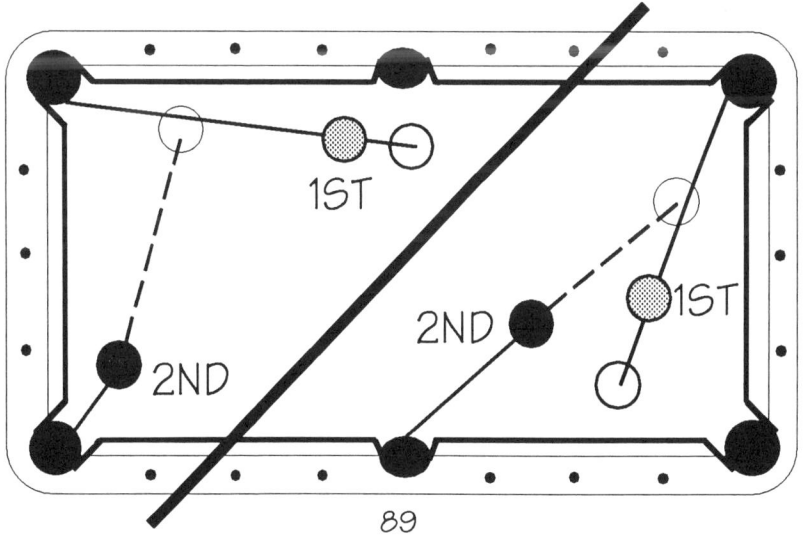

ALL ROADS LEAD TO THE SPOT

USE THE SAME AIMING SYSTEM - SPOT

THE HALF BALL AND STRAIGHT IN PLAYS ARE GREAT FOR BALL-IN-GRASP (HAND), BUT MOST OF YOUR OTHER PLAYS WILL BE VARIABLE CUTS. HERE ARE SOME TIPS FOR THOSE.

PIPER NOTE

A FATTER PLAY SLOWS THE CUE BALL'S SPEED AFTER IT CONTACTS THE OBJECT BALL, SO IT IS EASIER TO KNOW WHERE THE CUE BALL WILL COME TO REST. A THINNER PLAY STILL HAS ALOT OF ITS ORIGINAL SPEED SO IT IS EASIER TO MOVE THE CUE BALL AROUND THE TABLE.

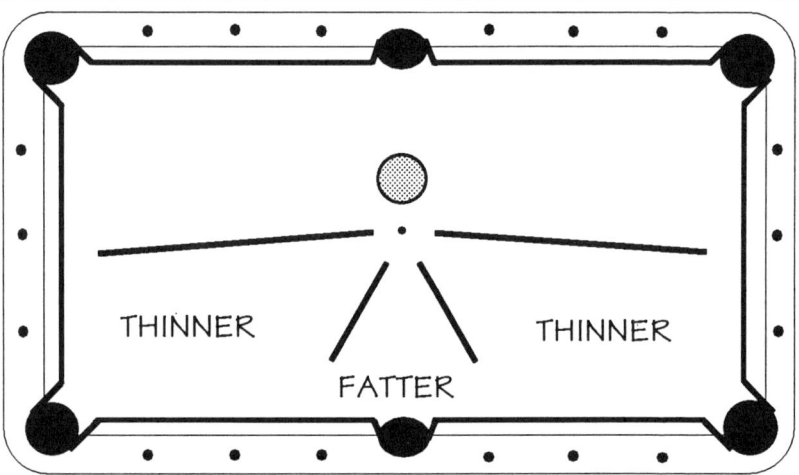

GET ROCKY ON THE RIGHT TRACK

THE TANGENT* RAILROAD-- A ROCKY ROAD

Bird's eye view, Spot is under Rocky's nose.

YOU CAN CHOOSE THE TRACK THAT ROCKY WILL TAKE FROM THE OBJECT BALL.
SPEED AND ROLL CHANGE ROCKY'S ROAD.

PIPER NOTE **IF THE CUE BALL SLIDES INTO THE OBJECT BALL--ROCKY TAKES THE TANGENT RAILROAD. IF THE CUE BALL ROLLS INTO THE OBJECT BALL--ROCKY ROLLS FORWARD OFF THE TANGENT LINE RAILROAD.**

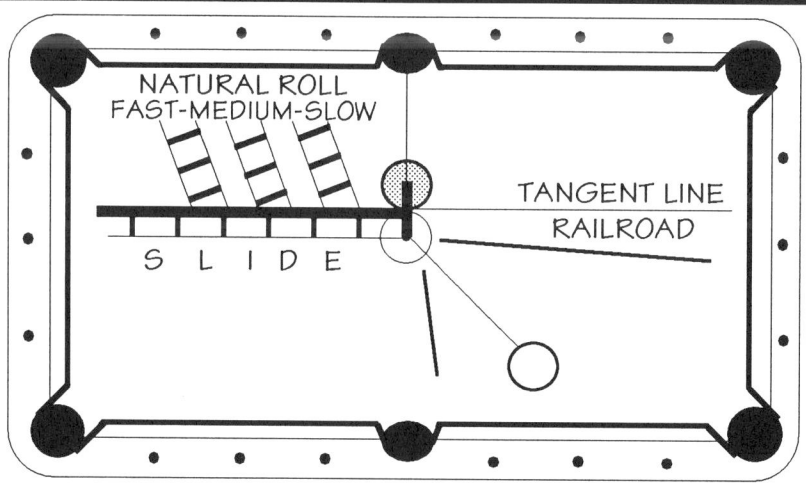

NATURAL ROLL
FAST-MEDIUM-SLOW

TANGENT LINE
RAILROAD

S L I D E

TWO BALL RUNS

HALF BALL SLIDE PLAYS

HERE ARE SOME EXAMPLES OF ROCKY
TAKING THE TANGENT LINE RAILROAD.

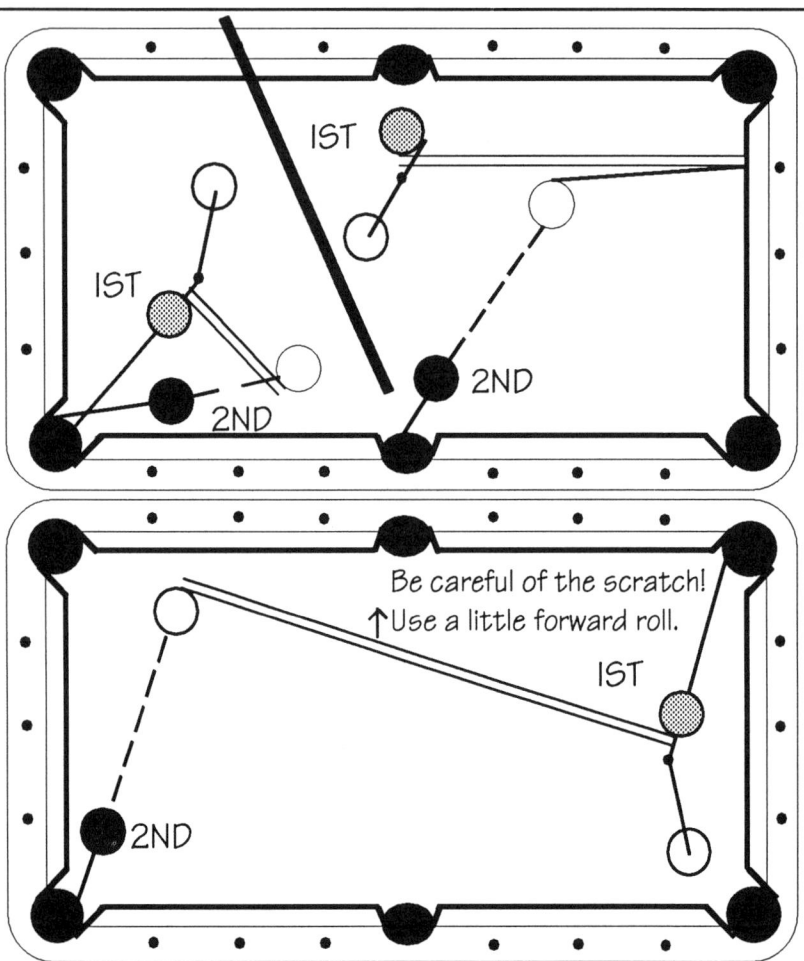

TWO BALL RUNS

HALF BALL FORWARD ROLL PLAY

HERE ARE SOME EXAMPLES OF ROCKY ROLLING
FORWARD OFF THE TANGENT LINE RAILROAD.
NOTE THE PIE'D PORTION OF THE TABLE BELOW..

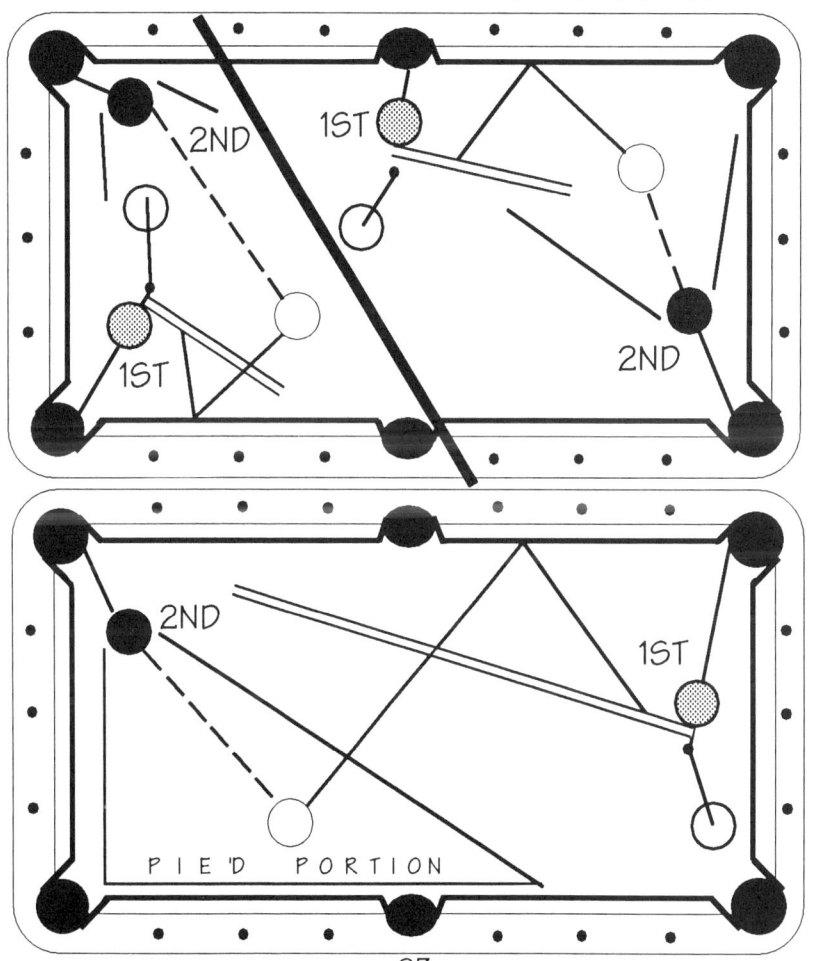

USING THE WHOLE POCKET

 HERE IS A GREAT WAY TO GET POSITION OR TO JUST AVOID A SCRATCH*. YOU CAN CHANGE THE PATH THE CUE BALL TAKES AFTER CONTACTING THE OBJECT BALL BY HAVING THE OBJECT BALL ENTER THE POCKET ON EITHER SIDE OF THE MIDDLE.

 PIPER NOTE **THE POCKET IS ABOUT TWO BALLS WIDE. YOU WANT TO BE ON EITHER SIDE OF THE CENTER OF THE TUNNEL OF SMILES TO ACHIEVE THE FOLLOWING RESULTS.**

POCKET TO THE LEFT (OF CENTER)-
- POCKET TO THE RIGHT-
- YOU ARE NOT STUCK IN THE MIDDLE ANYMORE.
TRY THIS ALL DIFFERENT WAYS SLOW,
MEDIUM AND FAST --SLIDING AND ROLLING.

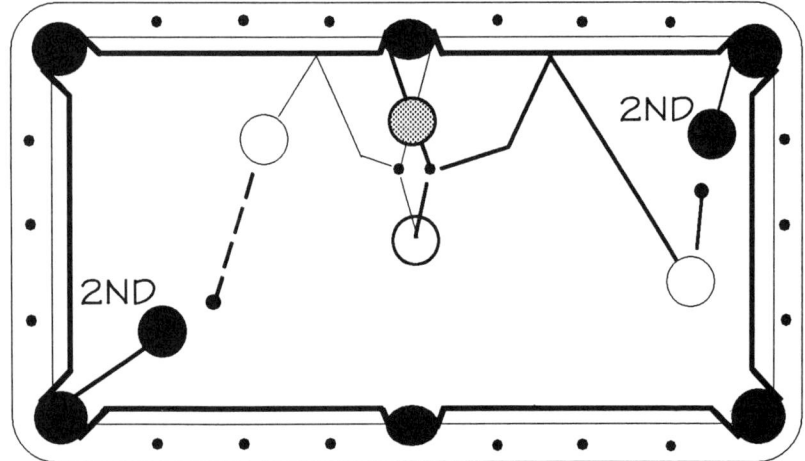

* THIRD WAY TO AVOID A SCRATCH.

CAN YOU SEE THE ℙ⊚SITION?

POSITION ROCKY FOR A HAPPY LANDING

PORTION: The pie'd part of the table where the Cue Ball needs to come to rest for a good next play.

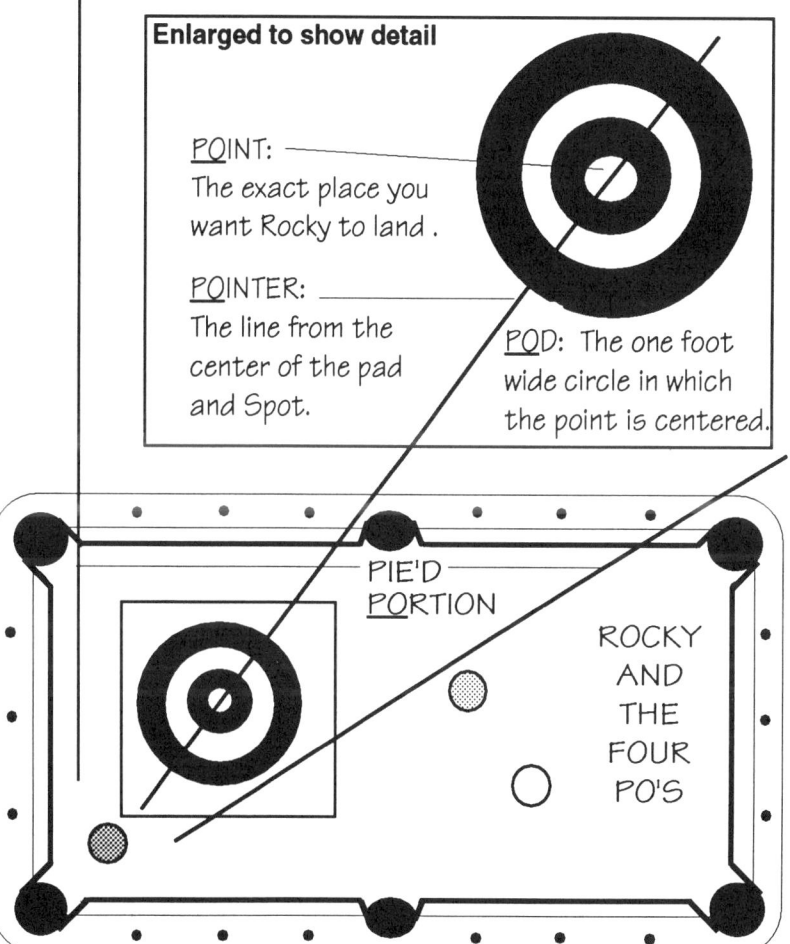

Enlarged to show detail

POINT:
The exact place you want Rocky to land .

POINTER:
The line from the center of the pad and Spot.

POD: The one foot wide circle in which the point is centered.

PIE'D
PORTION

ROCKY
AND
THE
FOUR
PO'S

THIN CUTS AND SPEED

NOT TOO MUCH SPEED--NOT TOO LITTLE SPEED

FOR GREAT POSITION PLAY ON A THIN CUT, YOU NEED TO TOSS AT THE RIGHT SPEED.

PIPER NOTE

THE CUT IS SO THIN THAT THE CUE BALL DOES NOT LOSE MUCH SPEED-- SO IT IS EASY TO DO EXAMPLE "A". YOU NEED TO TOSS FASTER FOR EXAMPLE "B" TO GET POSITION USING TWO RAILS.

NOTE: A IS TOP AND B IS BOTTOM

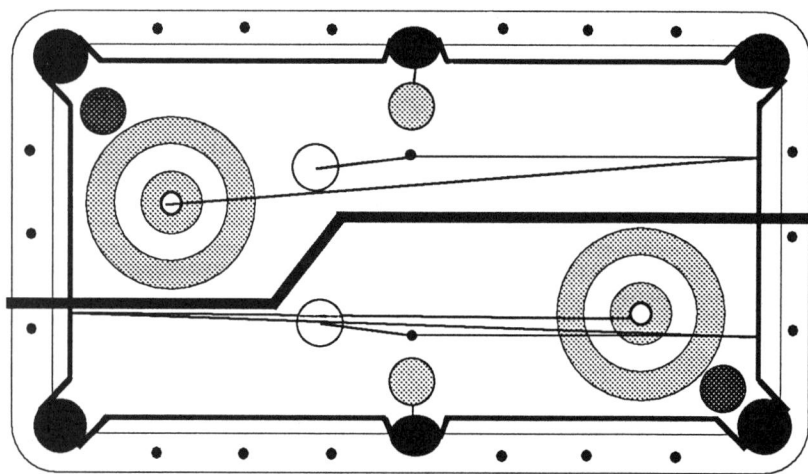

SLIDE AND ROLL MAKE ALMOST NO DIFFERENCE.

FAT CUTS AND SPEED

IF YOU CAN MAKE THE PLAY "EXAMPLE D" BELOW -- YOU ARE BECOMING QUITE A POOL PLAYER! YOU MAY HAVE TO CUE UP A little HIGHER ON ROCKY.

PIPER NOTE

THIS IS A FAT CUT WITH FORWARD ROLL WITH DIFFERENT SPEEDS. FOR "D" CUE UP A BIT LESS THAN 3/4 OF AN INCH ABOVE CENTER.

THE CUE BALL WILL COME TO REST AT...

"A"--   SLOW SPEED   FOR POSITION ON   a

"B"--   MEDIUM SPEED   FOR A SCRATCH   NO!

"C"--   MEDIUM+ SPEED   FOR POSITION ON   c

"D"--   FAST SPEED *   FOR SUPER "PO" ON   d

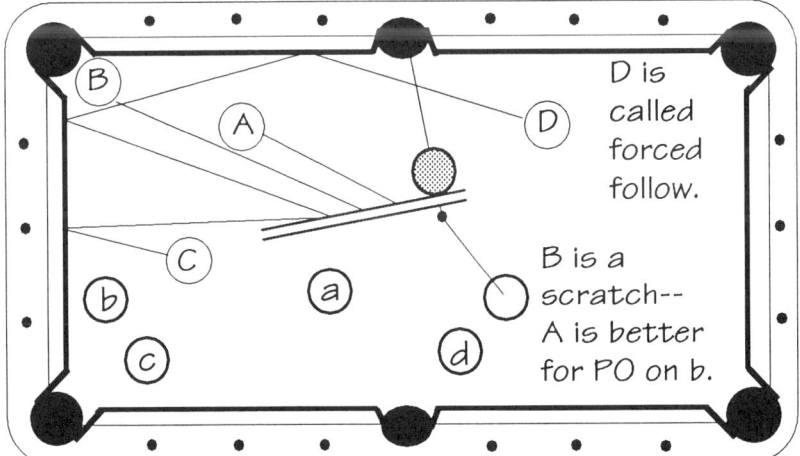

D is called forced follow.

B is a scratch-- A is better for PO on b.

* MOVE SPOT A DIME'S THICKNESS CLOSER TO THE OBJECT BALL WHEN TOSSING FAST.   97

BIGGEST MISTAKE IN POOL

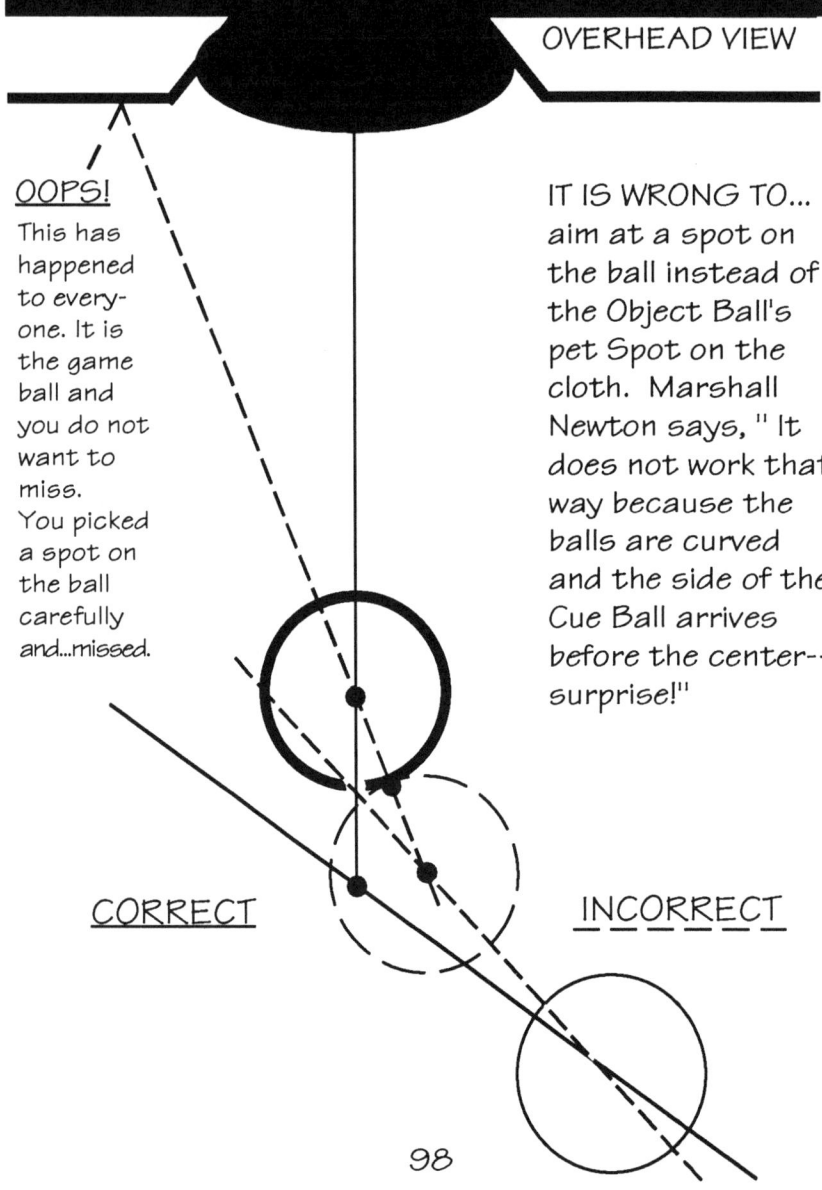

OVERHEAD VIEW

OOPS!
This has
happened
to every-
one. It is
the game
ball and
you do not
want to
miss.
You picked
a spot on
the ball
carefully
and...missed.

IT IS WRONG TO...
aim at a spot on
the ball instead of
the Object Ball's
pet Spot on the
cloth. Marshall
Newton says, " It
does not work that
way because the
balls are curved
and the side of the
Cue Ball arrives
before the center--
surprise!"

CORRECT   INCORRECT

SUMMARY

THEY USED TO CALL ME FATS --BUT I STARTED EATING RIGHT AND NOW THEY JUST CALL ME A GREAT POOL PLAYER. REMEMBER: AIM AT SPOT, WHERE THE IMAGINARY CUE BALL SHOULD BE WHEN IT CONTACTS THE OBJECT BALL. THE LINE THAT SPOT AND THE OBJECT BALL ARE ON IS THE CENTER LINE OF THE TUNNEL OF SMILES. REMEMBER: ROCK SLIDE SLIM STOPS ON SPOT--A STRAIGHT ON SHOT. HALF BALL SHOTS ARE THE MOST PLAYED SHOT IN POOL. ALL ROADS LEAD TO SPOT.

PIPER NOTE

Try to follow the same toss sequence every time you play. As you learn more--put it into your sequence. Do not get frustrated if you are missing. Figure out why you miss and fix it.

"EDDY CUT" OFFERS SHOTS ON ETIQUETTE

Food and drink put on the table can accidently stain or ruin the cloth. Do not put them on the table--use the ledges instead. It is also wise not to eat or drink over the table because someone might bump into you and it would spill.

the game of **EIGHTBALL**
Meet the Rack...

The Seven is Truthful.

BE TRUE TO YOURSELF, LEARN THIS!

This chapter is about the **BIGGEST SECRET** in the Land of Pool.

Things are not what they appear. The laws of physics prove it, and physics is the law in the Land of Pool.

My Name is... PLATO

IT'S THE TRUTH...
THIS IS ONE OF THE MANY WONDERS OF POOL

CHAPTER

THE BIG SECRET--CUT SHOT THROW

You would suspect that the Object Ball will follow the line from Spot through its center. This is not true, except for a perfectly straight play. In all other plays (cut shots) the Object Ball is thrown off line by the friction between the balls and the cloth and the friction between the balls themselves.

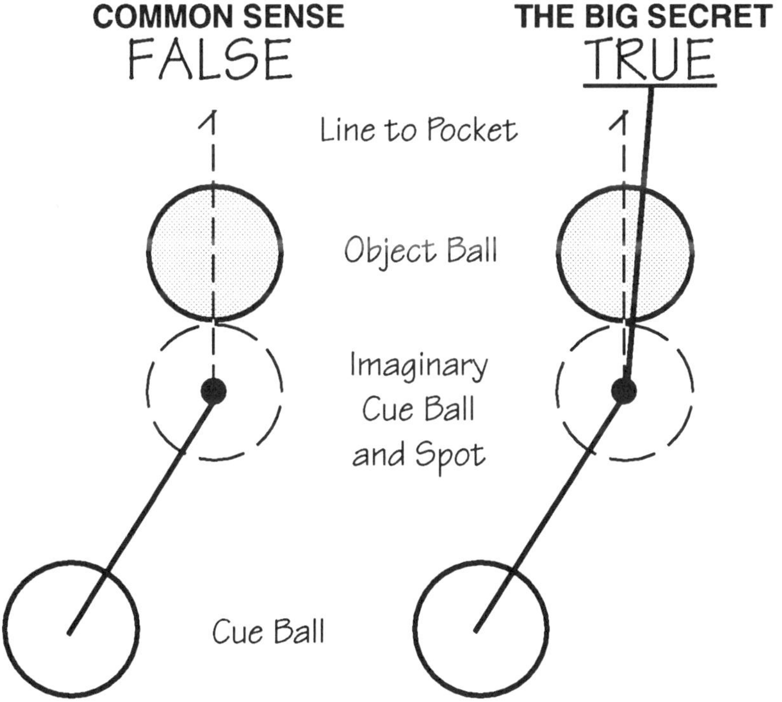

COMMON SENSE
FALSE

THE BIG SECRET
TRUE

Line to Pocket

Object Ball

Imaginary
Cue Ball
and Spot

Cue Ball

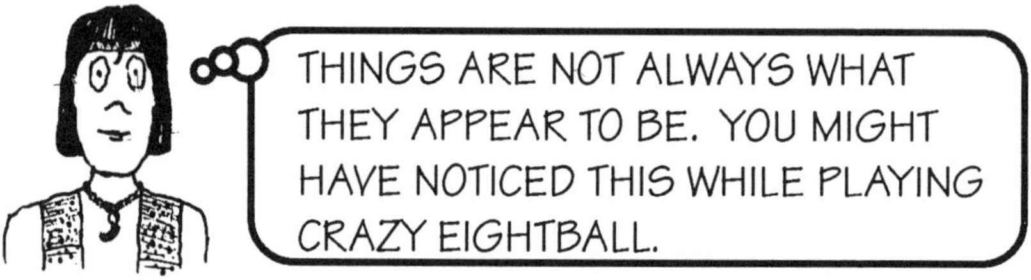

THINGS ARE NOT ALWAYS WHAT THEY APPEAR TO BE. YOU MIGHT HAVE NOTICED THIS WHILE PLAYING CRAZY EIGHTBALL.

PIPER NOTE

SET UP THIS THREE FOOT TO THE POCKET FROZEN COMBINATION. TRY IT FIVE TIMES ON EACH SIDE OF THE POCKET-- SLOW AND EASY TOSS WITH A NATURALLY ROLLING CUE BALL.

It does not look good but it is.

It looks good but it is not.

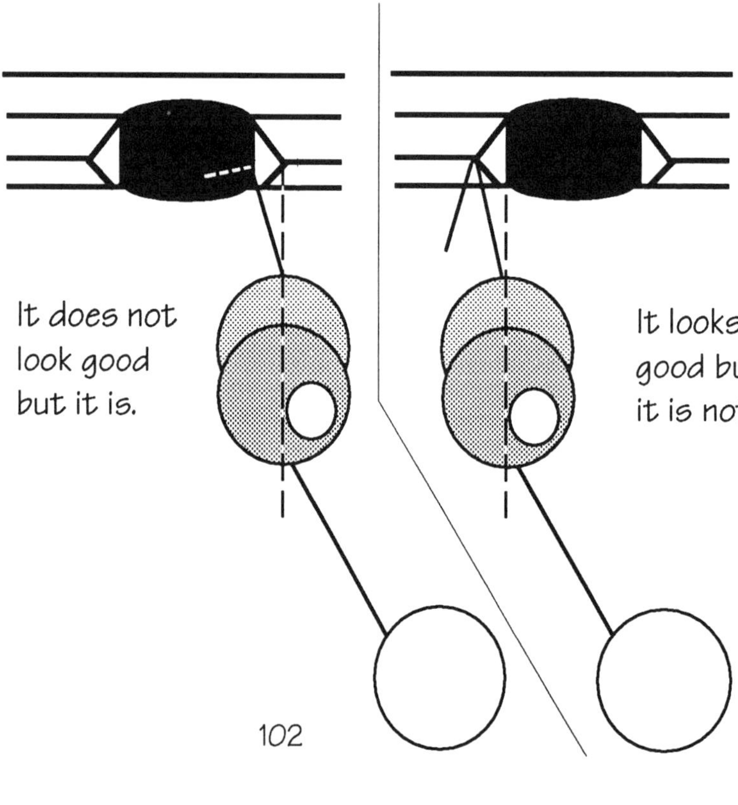

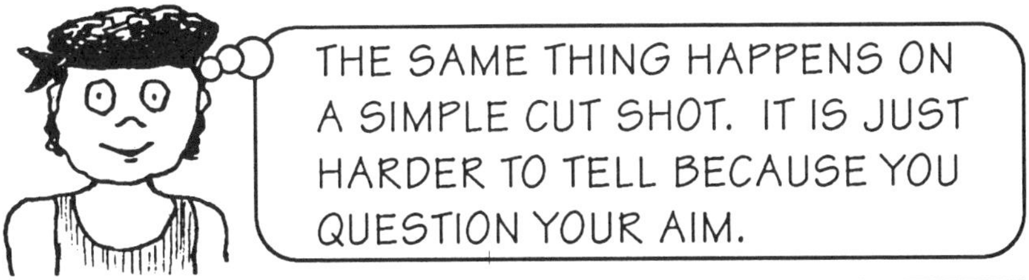

THE SAME THING HAPPENS ON A SIMPLE CUT SHOT. IT IS JUST HARDER TO TELL BECAUSE YOU QUESTION YOUR AIM.

PIPER NOTE

NOW, REMOVE THE BALL ON SPOT. FIND SPOT AND MAKE THE SAME PLAY. THE THROW IS ABOUT HALF BUT THE RESULTS ARE THE SAME. REMEMBER TO USE A NATURALLY ROLLING CUE BALL.

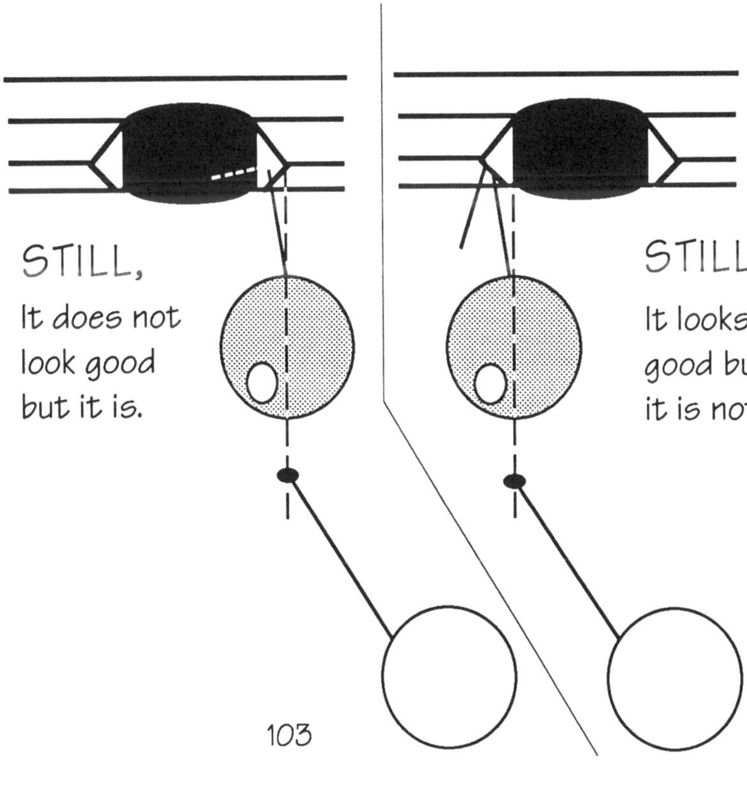

STILL,

It does not look good but it is.

STILL,

It looks good but it is not.

Hey, Piper, is this why I miss easy cut shots? I always seem to be on the far side of the pocket!

Set up this half ball shot so the footspot is Aim Spot--directly to the center of the Tunnel of Smiles.

PIPER NOTE

But, we just learned that with a naturally rolling Cue Ball the Object Ball will throw off line.

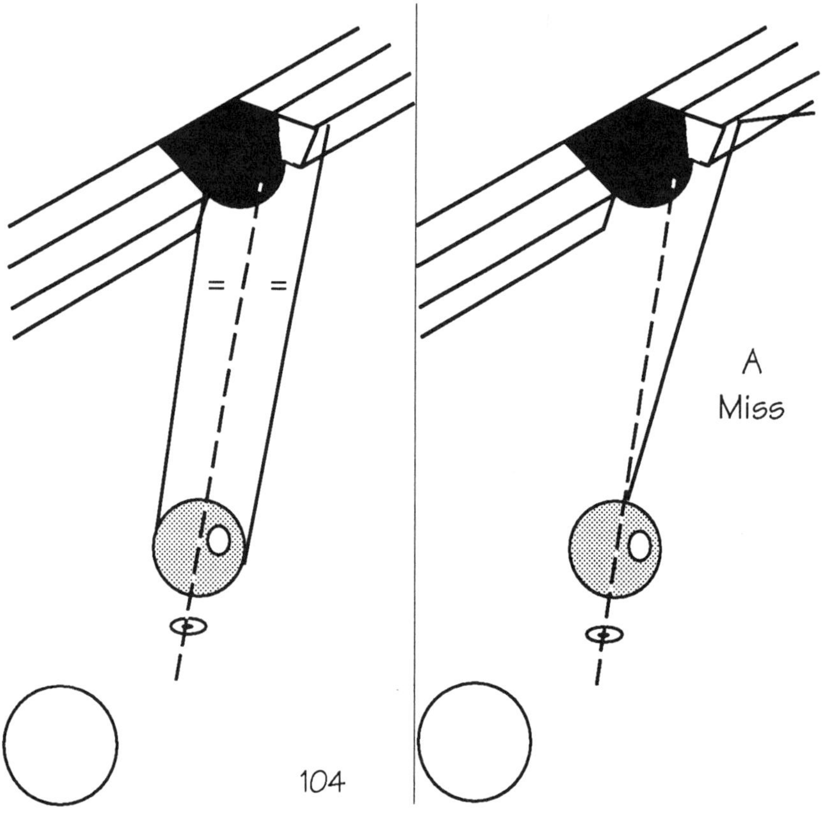

= / =

A Miss

ANSWER TO THROW IS CATCH!

MEET AIM SPOT'S COUSIN CATCH SPOT

Just adjust for the throw. Find the center line in the Tunnel of Smiles. <u>Move the point of entry into the pocket (for this example) 3/4 of a ball wide toward the CATCH LIP</u>. Find the new line from there through the Object Ball and find the CATCH SPOT.

AIM AT THE CATCH SPOT NOT THE AIM SPOT.

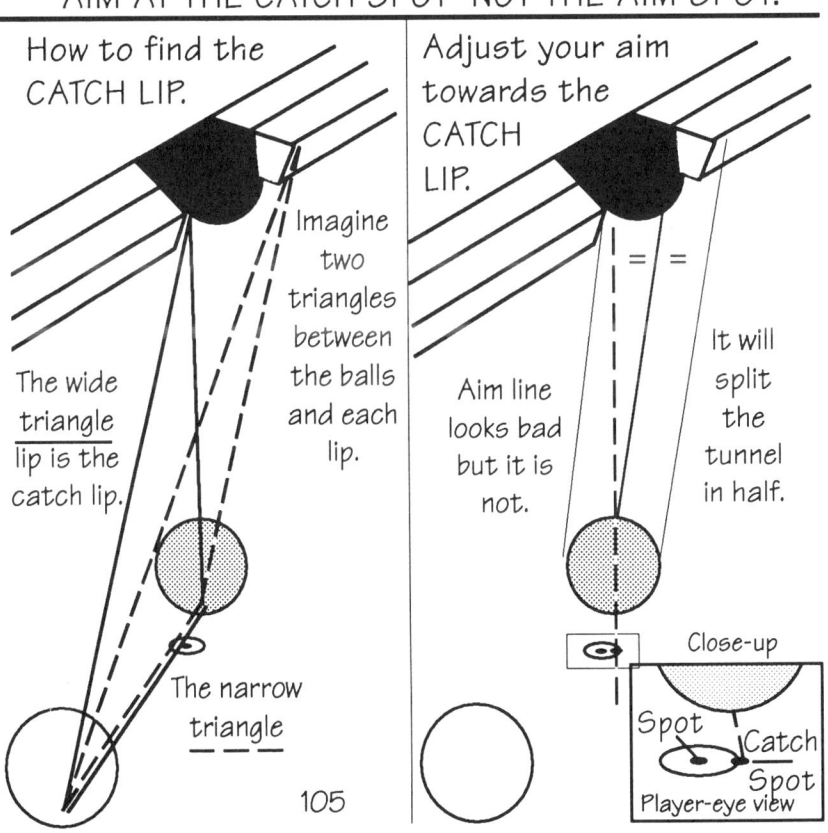

How to find the CATCH LIP.

The wide triangle <u>lip is the</u> catch lip.

Imagine two triangles between the balls and each lip.

The narrow triangle

Adjust your aim towards the CATCH LIP.

Aim line looks bad but it is not.

It will split the tunnel in half.

Close-up

Spot

Catch Spot

Player-eye view

105

BUT IT ALL KIND OF DEPENDS ON...

HOW ARE WE SUPPOSED TO KNOW HOW MUCH EVERY SHOT IS GOING TO THROW?

THE CHART ON THE NEXT PAGE WILL GIVE YOU A PLACE TO START. HOWEVER, IT VARIES ON EVERY TABLE AND IS DEPENDENT ON THE HUMIDITY.

PIPER NOTE

THE HUMIDITY, COME ON, WHAT IS HUMIDITY?

IT IS HOW MUCH MOISTURE IS IN THE AIR. MOISTURE ACTS AS A LUBRICANT BETWEEN THE BALLS THUS REDUCING THE FRICTION. LESS FRICTION, LESS THROW.

What is friction? Rub your hands together. After awhile they will get hot. Now wet your hands with cool water and rub them together. Your hands will take longer to get hot--less friction.

This is really easy to remember. You just have to know some simple division. After you learn this method this way it will become second nature--you will know instinctively how to adjust for Cut Shot Throw.

HOW TO USE THE BALL'S WIDTH AS A RULER

OBJECT BALL'S DISTANCE TO THE POCKET	BALL'S WIDTH AIM ADJUSTMENT
1 FOOT PLAY	1/4 BALL
2 FOOT PLAY	2/4 BALL
3 FOOT PLAY	3/4 BALL
4 FOOT PLAY	4/4 BALL
5 FOOT PLAY	5/4 BALL
6 FOOT PLAY	6/4 BALL

PIPER NOTE

JUST REMEMBER, THE OBJECT BALL'S DISTANCE TO THE POCKET IS DIVIDED INTO QUARTERS OF A BALL.

IF THE DISTANCE TO THE POCKET IS NOT AN EVEN NUMBER THEN ADJUST A BIT LESS OR MORE THAN THE CLOSEST ONE.

HERE ARE SOME GREAT WARM-UP TIPS. THE CUT SHOT THROW EFFECT VARIES FROM DAY-TO-DAY AND FROM TABLE TO TABLE. IT IS GOOD TO SEE HOW THE BALLS ARE THROWING TODAY.

1. Check to see if you are tossing straight--with the 7 out of 10 warm up , "Bounce Back".

2. Make sure to just roll the ball back to your tip. Use just enough speed. Do this widthwise and then lengthwise on the table.

3. Set up the shot below and get a feel for the throw, today. You will be surprised how much it can vary.

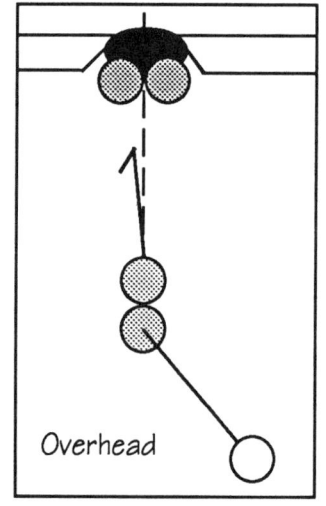

Overhead

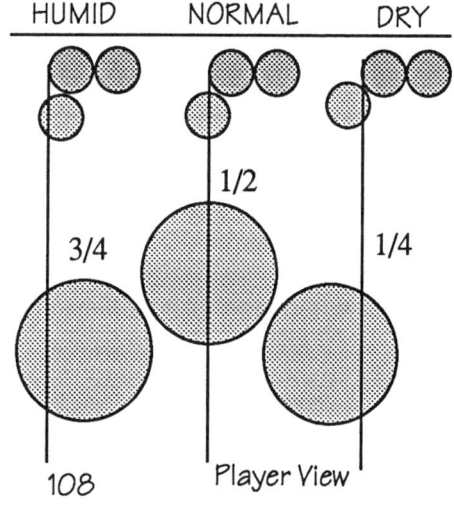

HUMID   NORMAL   DRY

1/2

3/4   1/4

Player View

SUMMARY

Now you know pool's BIG secret.
Here are some more tips:
The faster you toss, the less the throw.
The slower you toss, the more the throw.
The fatter the cut, the less the throw.
The thinner the cut, the more the throw.
The higher the humidity, the less the throw.
The lesser humidity, the more the throw.

Remember: Faster-Wetter-Fatter is less
and Slower-Dryer-Thinner is more.

PIPER
NOTE

Most tables come with a ruler at the pocket to help adjust for throw. Look for the worn lines on the cloth which the pocketed balls made over time. The distance from the line to the rail is about half (2/4ths) of a ball wide.

"EDDY CUT" OFFERS SHOTS ON ETIQUETTE

Yelling, screaming, loud talking or singing will disturb the other players. Be Cool so everyone playing in the room will have a good time!

FOR GOODNESS SAKE –

CONCENTRATE!

CHAPTER

MORE GREAT CONCEPT BALLS

THE BLOCKED BALL: This is a team ball that is blocked to its only clear pocket by a member of its own team. Pocket the Blocker to get to the Blocked Ball.

THE DUCK GOALIE BALL: Why a duck? If a ball from your team is sitting in the jaws of a pocket--leave it for last. It is now your pocket.

THE BREAK BALL: This is the most clever concept of all. While pocketing this ball the Cue Ball takes a track that knocks your Trouble Ball out of trouble. They are especially useful with Ball-in-Hand plays.

THE DUNCE BALL: You heard of this one in theory earlier. If you move your friend's Trouble Ball out of trouble, that was your Dunce Ball. That is your friend's job.

ANOTHER GREAT CONCEPT BALL

THE DUCK BALL
OR
SOME WAYS TO PLAY A DUCK

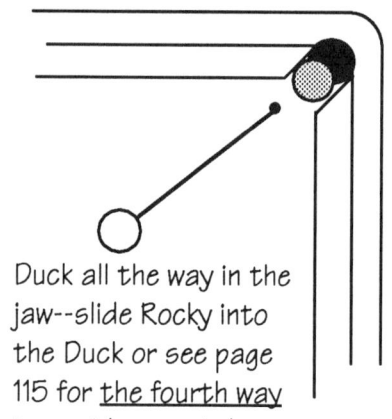

Duck all the way in the jaw--slide Rocky into the Duck or see page 115 for <u>the fourth way</u> to avoid a scratch.

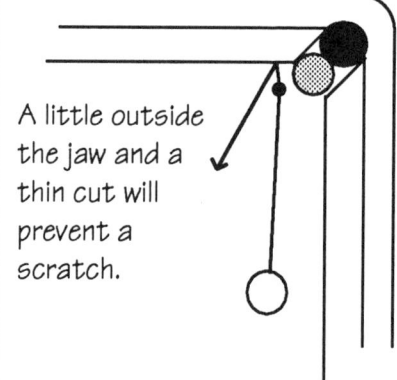

A little outside the jaw and a thin cut will prevent a scratch.

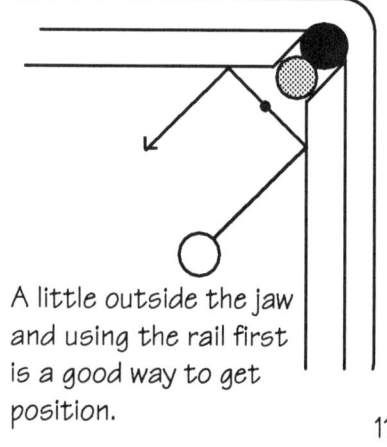

A little outside the jaw and using the rail first is a good way to get position.

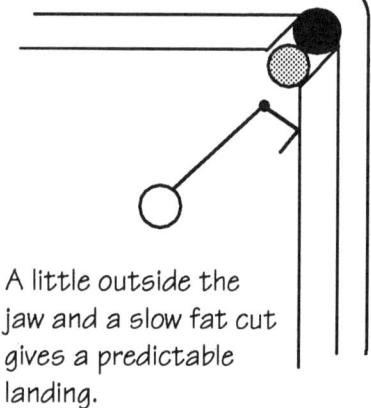

A little outside the jaw and a slow fat cut gives a predictable landing.

BRIDGES FOR TROUBLED SHOTS

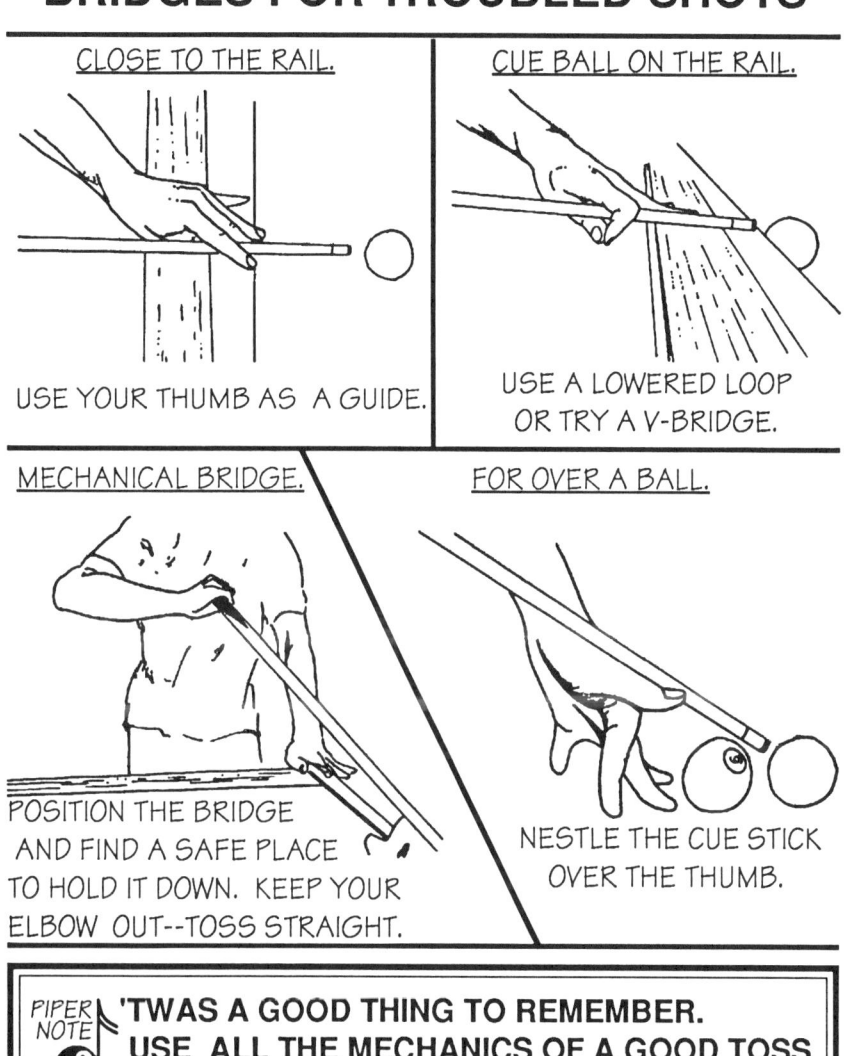

CLOSE TO THE RAIL.

USE YOUR THUMB AS A GUIDE.

CUE BALL ON THE RAIL.

USE A LOWERED LOOP
OR TRY A V-BRIDGE.

MECHANICAL BRIDGE.

POSITION THE BRIDGE
AND FIND A SAFE PLACE
TO HOLD IT DOWN. KEEP YOUR
ELBOW OUT--TOSS STRAIGHT.

FOR OVER A BALL.

NESTLE THE CUE STICK
OVER THE THUMB.

PIPER NOTE 'TWAS A GOOD THING TO REMEMBER.
USE ALL THE MECHANICS OF A GOOD TOSS
WHEN USING THESE DIFFICULT BRIDGES

HOW TO MAKE A CLOSED BRIDGE

IT IS AN O.K. METHOD.

1.

Make the International O.K. sign
with your bridge hand.
This is what you see.

2.

Now put it down on the table.
Spread out the "K"--your fingers.
Keep the "O" connected.

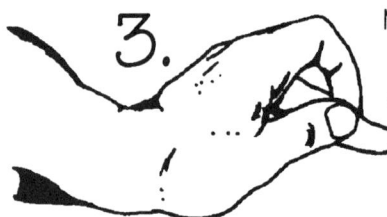

3.

Now connect the "O" and the "K"
by supporting the "O" on the
side of the middle finger. Make
sure it is firmly attached.

Insert the Cue Stick
through the "O".
It should be held
firmly in place--
by having the Cue
Stick supported top,
bottom and both
sides by the fingers.

4.

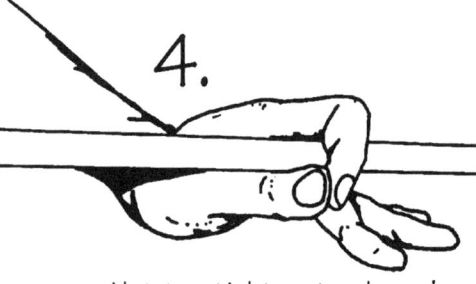

Not too tight or too loose!

HOW TO APPLY BACKSPIN

Here are a few simple things to remember to get great backspin.

1. ALWAYS chalk up before a backspin play.

2. LOOSEN up. You do not have to power through the Cue Ball.

3. Toss your WRIST as well as your forearm.

4. Make sure to FOLLOW THROUGH!

5. Always use a CLOSED bridge.

Piper, I am afraid I will hurt the cloth. The Cue Stick seems to want to brush the cloth on these plays.

 PIPER NOTE **IT'S O.K., JUST MAKE SURE TO TOSS THE CUE STICK STRAIGHT. JUST DON'T JUMP UP--STAY DOWN.**

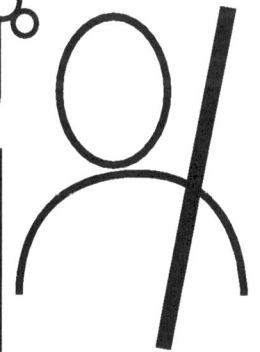

TWO   BALL   RUNS

STRAIGHT-IN BACKSPIN PLAY

IF THE CUE BALL ARRIVES AT THE OBJECT BALL; ROLLING IT IS ALSO CALLED FOLLOW; SLIDING IS ALSO CALLED STUN; BACKSPINNING IS ALSO CALLED DRAW.

PIPER NOTE

DRAW IS EASY TO CONTROL IF YOU TOSS SLOW AND CONTACT THE CUE BALL LOW. HOWEVER, THE FASTER YOU TOSS THE CUE THE HARDER IT IS TO KNOW WHERE THE CUE BALL WILL END UP. YOU CAN INCREASE THE AMOUNT OF DRAW BY EITHER CONTACTING THE CUE BALL LOWER OR TOSSING FASTER OR A COMBINATION OF BOTH.

TWO IN ONE SHOT

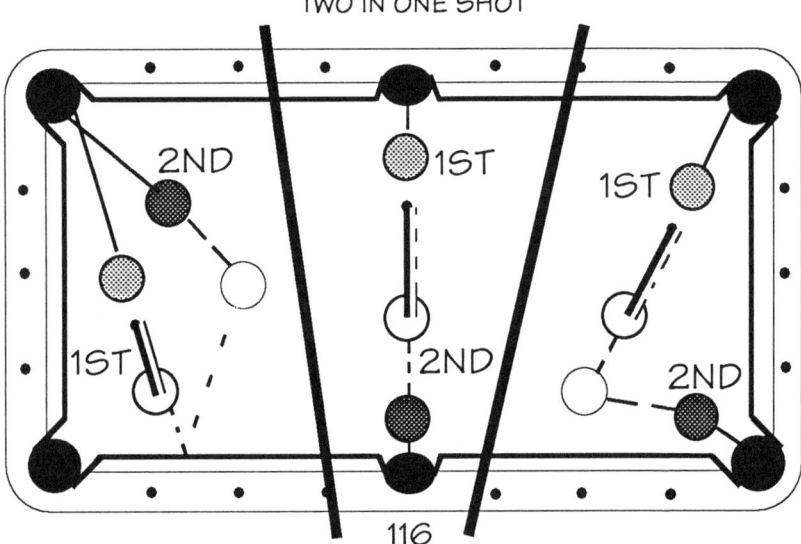

116

TWO BALL RUNS

HALF BALL BACKSPIN PLAY

DRAW REDUCES THE THROW EFFECT. EXPERIMENT WITH HALF THE AMOUNT OF THROW AND ADJUST. THE BACK-SPIN ON THE CUE BALL PICKS THE OBJECT BALL UP OFF THE CLOTH A LITTLE--REDUCING THE FRICTION.

PIPER NOTE

IN THIS EXAMPLE, DRAW SEEMS TO BE THE EASIEST WAY TO GET POSITION. HOWEVER, FOLLOW IS THE BEST ANSWER BECAUSE ROCKY WILL BE IN THE PIE'D PORTION THE LONGEST TIME. "D" IS FOR DRAW AND "F" IS FOR FOLLOW.

NOTE: BACKSPIN BRINGS ROCKY BACK OFF THE TANGENT LINE.

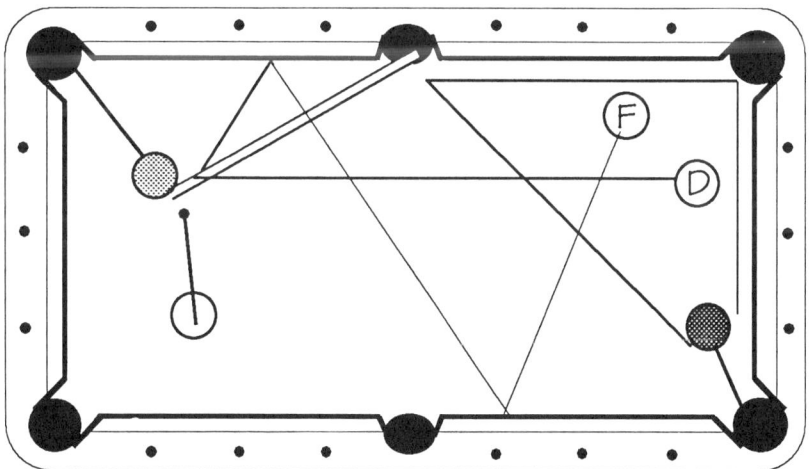

THE TANGENT RAILROAD IS A SCRATCH--DO NOT USE SLIDE.

POSITION PRACTICE
WHO NOSE WHERE ROCKY GOES?

 BY USING THIS CHART COMBINED WITH A STEADY SPEED YOU CAN GET TO ANY POSITION ON THE NEXT PAGE.

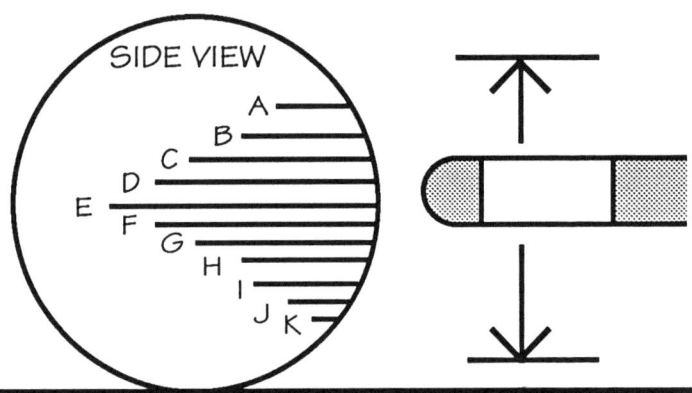

SIDE VIEW

A
B
C
D
E
F
G
H
I
J K

PIPER NOTE **REMEMBER, KEEP YOUR CUE AS LEVEL AS POSSIBLE. TO REACH E-K MAKE SURE TO FOLLOW THROUGH, LOWER YOUR BRIDGE AND SNAP YOUR WRIST.**

 BAD PUN, PIPER!

GET YOUR P○ TOGETHER

THIS IS HOW IT'S DONE!

POSITION PLAY
IS REALLY NEAT .
I CAN MOVE THE CUE BALL
AROUND THE TABLE
REALLY WELL.

PIPER
NOTE

THIS DIAGRAM SHOWS A
SEEMINGLY STRAIGHT-IN PLAY.
BY **USING THE POCKET**, AND APPLYING
DRAW, FOLLOW AND STUN-
-YOU CAN MOVE THE CUE BALL
ANYWHERE ON THE TABLE BY
VARYING THE **SPEED** YOU TOSS THE CUE.

YOU CAN GET ANYWHERE FROM HERE!

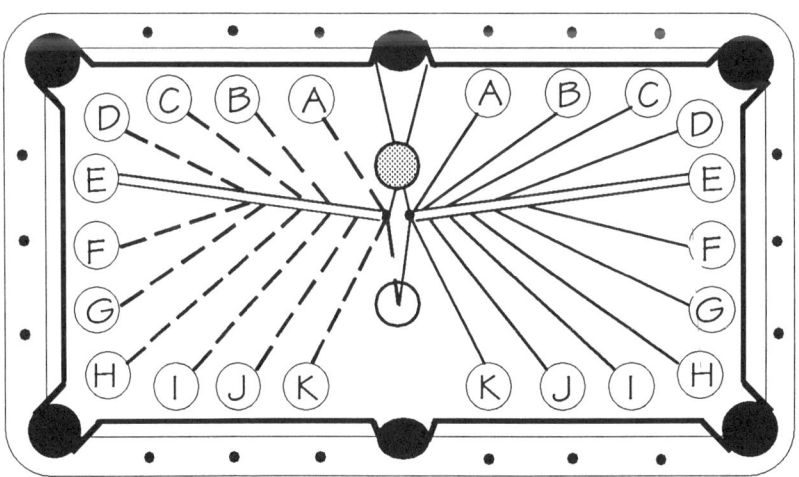

REMEMBER THE BREAK--

IF YOU HAVE A CHOICE TAKE SOLIDS.

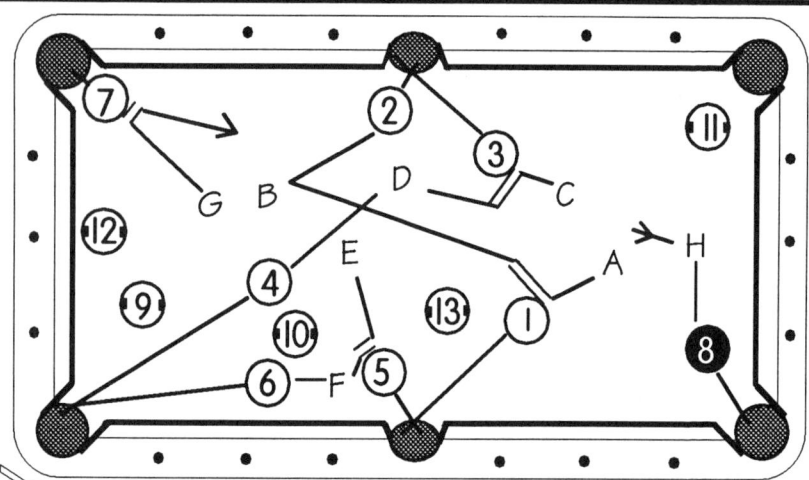

FIRST TWO BALL RUN: START AT "A" FOR THE
ONE IN THE SIDE, PLAYED WITH A SLOW NATURALLY
ROLLING BALL FOR PO "B" ON THE TWO IN THE SIDE.

NEXT TWO BALL RUN: START AT "C" FOR THE THREE
IN THE SIDE WITH A SLOW NATURALLY ROLLING BALL
FOR PO "D" ON THE FOUR IN THE CORNER.
(DON'T MOVE THE TEN BALL OUT OF TROUBLE!)

NEXT TWO BALL RUN: START AT "E" FOR THE
FIVE IN THE SIDE PLAYED WITH VERY SLOW ROLL
FOR PO "F" ON THE SIX IN THE CORNER.

LAST TWO BALL RUN: START AT "G" FOR THE SEVEN
IN THE CORNER PLAYED WITH A LOT OF DRAW FOR
PO "H" ON THE EIGHTBALL IN THE CORNER.

120

--IN CHAPTER FIVE?

IF YOU GET STUCK WITH STRIPES.

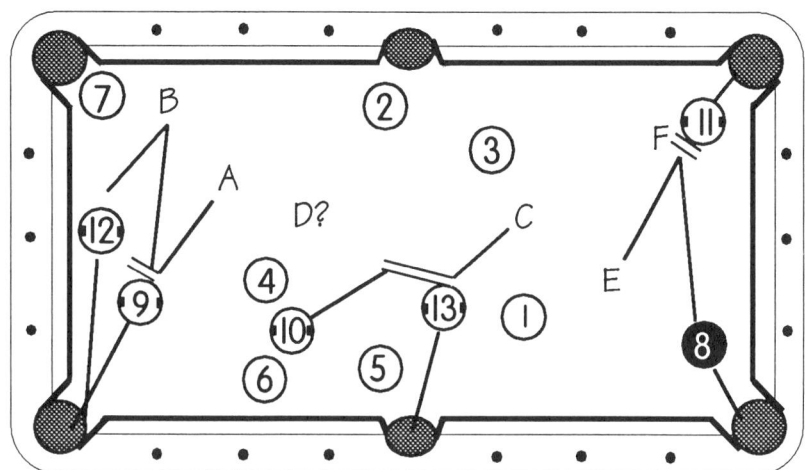

FIRST UNBLOCK THE BLOCKED BALL: START AT "A"
FOR THE NINE IN THE CORNER, PLAYED WITH DRAW
TO COME BACK FOR THE TWELVE IN THE NOW
UNBLOCKED CORNER.

THE BREAK BALL: START AT "C" FOR THE THIRTEEN IN
THE SIDE WITH A NATURALLY ROLLING BALL TO
BREAK OUT THE TEN BALL. YOU MAY END UP WITH A
SHOT ON THE TEN IF YOU ARE LUCKY. IF YOU PLAY
THIS TWO BALL RUN FIRST YOU MIGHT DISTURB THE
EASY NINE-TWELVE.

LAST TWO BALL RUN: START AT "E" FOR THE ELEVEN
IN THE CORNER.   A STOP SHOT FOR PO "F" ON THE
EIGHT FOR THE CORNER.

STRIPED LOGIC

EIGHTBALL FOUL SUMMARY

YOU LOSE YOUR TURN :

1. When you scratch or foul on your play. If any of your friend's team are pocketed --they remain pocketed. If any of your team are pocketed--they get spotted. Spotted means it is put on the footspot or longstring as close to the footspot as possible.

2. When you touch any other ball on the table with any part of your body or Cue Stick.

3. In Crazy Eightball Part One no fouls are called. In Crazy Eightball Part II the Cue Ball must touch the Eightball first. In the rest of the Crazy Eightball Games, the Cue Ball must touch a member of your team first.

4. When you miscue. When the tip of your Cue Stick touches the Cue Ball you have made your play. You may, however, adjust your Cue Ball-In-Hand plays with the ferrule or guide--just not the tip.

5. When you scratch on a Break, all balls pocketed remain so (except the Eightball which is spotted.) The next player has Cue Ball-in-Hand anywhere on the table for Parts One and II. For Parts III, IV and V it is Cue Ball-in-Hand in the Kitchen.

6. You lose the game when you pocket the Eightball in any pocket other than the called pocket. The Eightball has to be the Object Ball--The first ball contacted. All of your team must already be pocketed. NOTE: Scratching or fouling on the Eightball is not a loss--the next player gets Cue Ball-in-Hand (if the Eightball pockets and you scratch or foul--you lose).

CRAZY EIGHTBALL SUMMARY

PART ONE: BALL-IN-HAND EVERY SHOT
Use the Eightball as the Pretend Cue Ball and freeze the Cue Ball to the Object Ball on Spot. Pocket your whole team and then just pocket shoot the Eightball in the called pocket to win.

PART TWO: BALL-IN-HAND EVERY SHOT
Use the Cue Ball as the Cue Ball and freeze the Eightball to the Object Ball on Spot. To win, you must use the Cue Ball to pocket the Eightball.

PART THREE: BALL-IN-HAND EVERY SHOT
You must pocket your whole team using the Cue Ball. To win you must pocket the Eightball with a half ball shot.

PART FOUR: BALL-IN-GRASP EVERY OTHER SHOT
Grasp your B-I-G Opportunity to use Cue Ball-in-Grasp (Hand) to get POsition on your second shot. To win you must play the Eightball from where the Cue Ball lies. No Ball-in-Hand unless your friend fouls.

NEW! PART FIVE: BALL-IN-GRASP EACH INNING
You only get Ball-In-Grasp (Hand) at the start of your turn.

123

THOUGHT FOR FORETHOUGHT

DO NOT FORGET TO GIVE THOUGHT BEFORE YOU TOSS

Fourteen　Ball

My name is
FORETHOUGHT
I am for thoughtfulness.

NEVER FORGET TO...

...Find the easiest two ball run.
...Choose what POsition to get on the second ball.
...Find the right POrtion, POint, POinter and POd.
...Use the whole pocket to get good position.
...Choose the right speed of toss .
...Allow for throw based on the throw ruler.
...Decide whether to use stun, follow or draw.
...Then find Spot or Catch Spot.

...Before you set up to toss the Cue Stick.

Also...never forget to recycle the way you should, I am
a green ball and I am for Ecology.
　　　　　Please don't covet my tusks.

THE REST OF THE RACK

YOU HAVE EARNED YOUR LAST TWO STRIPES

Fifteen Ball

DO NOT FORGET
THE OTHER THREE BIGGIES!
1. THE BIG SECRET, CHAPTER 7.
2. THE BIG MISTAKE, PAGE 98.
3. THE B-I-G OPPORTUNITY PAGE 88.

My name is
BIGGIE
I am for big thinking.

Nine Ball

IN THE NEXT BOOK--I WILL TEACH YOU TO PLAY
NINEBALL. YOU HAVE NINE LIVES OR NINE
CHANCES TO POCKET ME TO WIN. YOU'LL
HAVE TO PAY EVEN MORE ATTENTION TO THE
TANGENT LINE RAILROAD ON EVERY PLAY.

My name is
NINE T'S
I am independent.

PIPER NOTE

**TALCUM POWDER HELPS THE CUE STICK GLIDE
SMOOTHLY THROUGH YOUR BRIDGE. IF YOU USE
TOO MUCH THOUGH, IT CAN HURT THE CLOTH.
ONLY BABIES LEAVE A TALC MESS. YOU MAY
WANT TO TRY A THREE FINGERED GLOVE, INSTEAD.**

SUMMARY

Sometimes things are hard to learn. With practice, if you apply yourself, you will understand these things and wonder why it was so hard to learn. Most pool games are won with the mind not the toss. Remember: Don't forget the strategy of a Blocked Ball, Dunce Ball, Duck Goalie and the Amazing Break Ball. Watch out for a potential scratch by looking for the Tangent Line Railroad.

PIPER NOTE **Play Two Ball as a solitary game. Toss one team ball on the table with the Eightball. With Ball-in-Grasp (Hand) on the team ball, run the two balls. BONUS: Draw reduces Cut Shot Throw by about half.**

"EDDY CUT" OFFERS SHOTS ON ETIQUETTE

Say, "Nice PO" to your friend when they land in the portion, at the point, on the pointer or the pod!

HOW TO BREAK

PIN MY NOSE RIGHT ON THE CENTER. CONTACT THE LEAD BALL OF THE RACK AS A STRAIGHT ON PLAY--NO MATTER WHERE IN THE KITCHEN YOU ARE TOSSING. I SHOULD END UP IN THE MIDDLE OF THE TABLE AFTER THE BREAK. THAT WAY YOU HAVE LOTS OF GOOD CHOICES FOR YOUR NEXT TOSS.

PIPER NOTE

FOR A GREAT BREAK SHOT, TOSS SMOOTH AND FAST. IF YOU TRY TO POWER THROUGH THE TOSS IT WILL BE JERKY AND THE BREAK WILL NOT BE GOOD.
YOUR BRIDGE SHOULD BE LONGER THAN NORMAL AND GRIP A LITTLE FURTHER BACK. LUCK PLAYS A BIG PART IN BREAKING SO DON'T GET DISCOURAGED.

POOL'S HOME *RUN*

IF YOU HAVE A TWO BALL RUN OR MORE THAT INCLUDES THE EIGHTSTER TO WIN-- YOU RAN OUT TO WIN. THAT IS THE SAME AS A HOME RUN IN BASEBALL. IF YOU RUN ALL YOUR TEAM AND THE EIGHTSTER IN ONE INNING--YOU HAD A GRAND RUN OUT. THAT IS THE SAME AS A GRAND SLAM IN BASEBALL! WOW! WRITE TO THE PIPER AND TELL HIM WHEN YOU HAD YOUR FIRST GRAND RUN OUT.

I hope you have enjoyed your time in the Land of Pool. PO is a great word from this Land. PO has many meanings. PO is for **potential,** which is what you have and will be if you try. PO is for **Pool,** a great sport. PO is for **positive** thinking, the key to achieving your goals. PO is for **potion,** the magic kind, the recipe being practice. PO is for **portion,** the pie'd part of the table to give you a good

play. PO is for **pointer,** the exact line on which you want the Cue Ball to land. PO is for **point,** the exact spot for the Cue Ball to land. PO is for landing **pod,** the one foot circle around the point. PO is for **position** play, which is what it is all about, pal. PO is also for **poo,** that's what happens when your friend does not leave you a shot. PO is for **pontificate,** which I hope is not what has happened here.

EPILOGUE

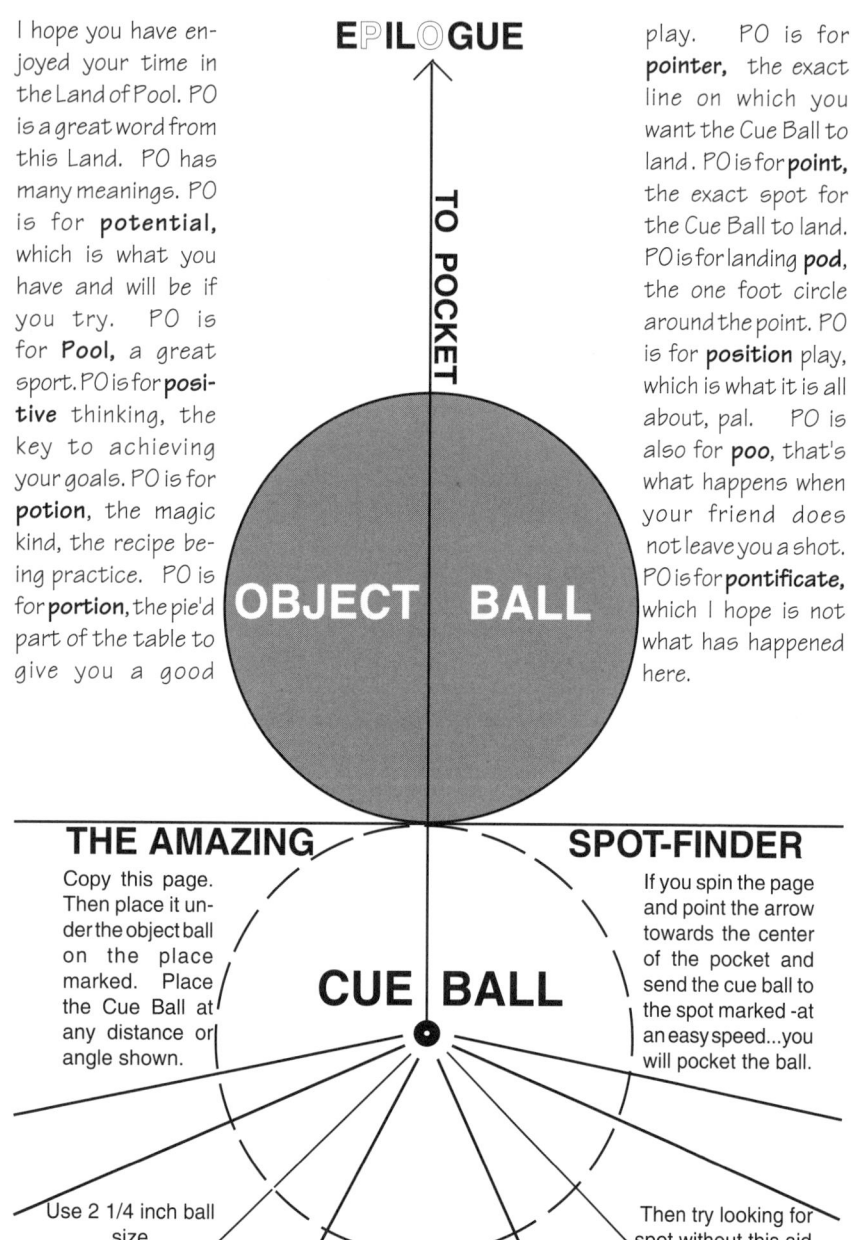

TO POCKET

OBJECT BALL

THE AMAZING

Copy this page. Then place it under the object ball on the place marked. Place the Cue Ball at any distance or angle shown.

SPOT-FINDER

If you spin the page and point the arrow towards the center of the pocket and send the cue ball to the spot marked -at an easy speed...you will pocket the ball.

CUE BALL

Use 2 1/4 inch ball size

Then try looking for spot without this aid.